"I had not finished reading the introduction to this book before I was making a mental list of friends that I knew would find it a balm to their weary hearts. Kristen and Sarah minister to fellow travelers on the road of suffering, out of the resources they have received on their own journeys, from the God of all comfort, grace, and hope."

**Nancy DeMoss Wolgemuth**, author; Host/Teacher of *Revive Our Hearts*

"Kristen and Sarah have let us in to listen to their meditations in the midst of pain and limitation. They've opened up their hearts, their stories, and their Word-filled words. From our various contexts, we will all learn as we listen. I'm grateful for this book's faithful call to lift up our eyes to a God of mercy who loves and saves."

**Kathleen Nielson**, Director of Women's Initiatives, The Gospel Coalition

"This is a wonderful, vulnerable and honest book, and I highly recommend it to anyone who needs the good news of Jesus in a difficult time. Kristen and Sarah have suffered immensely, but both of them know that our only hope is found in Jesus."

**Dave Furman**, Senior Pastor of Redeemer Church, Dubai; author of *Being There: How to Love Those Who are Hurting*

"We have been told that we can do anything, to dream big, because women are strong and capable. But what happens when you are confronted with your limitations in the form of suffering? When you feel weak and weary? Kristen and Sarah provide hope in your desperation, and they drive us to the cross of Christ, where all of our suffering makes sense."

**Courtney Reissig**, author of *The Accidental Feminist*

"Pain is a place where hope grows best, and this book will convince you of that. From beginning to end, *Hope When It Hurts* invites you to see the light of Jesus in the darkest times. As you turn each new page, listen for the voice of God, and you'll hear him cheering for you."

**Karl Clauson**, Radio Host at Moody Radio; author of *Thrill: When Normal is Not Enough*

"If you are in the midst of suffering, or someday will be (and that means us all), you will do well to read this book. I found myself moved, reflecting, and re-engaging with the truth of the gospel in the context of my own suffering. The whole book is full of empathy, a "coming alongside" tone, and insight for your soul."

**Josh Moody**, Senior Pastor, College Church, Wheaton

"In a style as comforting as a hand-delivered casserole, on pages as beautiful as the message you'll find written on each page, this book will drive you to the gospel again and again, lifting your eyes toward the only source of lasting hope. Keep your copy close—you'll find yourself running to it again and again."

**Erin Davis**, author of *Connected* and *Beyond Bath Time*

"Kristen and Sarah speak with fresh voices formed by their love of Scripture and their experience of walking with God through suffering. The faith and courage I've seen in them will overflow on you as you read this soothing and insightful book, giving you strength to stay the course even when you are tired of the battle."

**Colin Smith**, Senior Pastor, The Orchard Church;
President, Unlocking the Bible

"It's great to have a book written by people who are still in the thick of suffering, which shows us how to apply the gospel to our struggles so that we can persevere and also grow through them. Honest but not self-focused, this will be an invaluable resource to those in the midst of suffering and to those who seek to support and encourage them."

**Barbara Sherwood**, London Women's Convention Committee

"This isn't a collection of slogans and Christian jargon. It's biblical reflections from the heart of two women who have trusted Jesus in the hurts of their own lives. This is refreshingly honest, never condescending, never canned, and always gospel-focused."

**Dan DeWitt**, author of *Jesus or Nothing*

KRISTEN WETHERELL
& SARAH WALTON

Hope
when it
hurts

BIBLICAL REFLECTIONS TO HELP YOU GRASP
GOD'S PURPOSE IN YOUR SUFFERING

Hope When It Hurts

© Kristen Wetherell / Sarah Walton /
   The Good Book Company, 2017. Reprinted 2017 (twice).

Published by:
The Good Book Company

Tel (US): 866 244 2165
Tel (UK): 0333 123 0880
Email (US): info@thegoodbook.com
Email (UK): info@thegoodbook.co.uk

Websites:

North America: www.thegoodbook.com
UK: www.thegoodbook.co.uk
Australia: www.thegoodbook.com.au
New Zealand: www.thegoodbook.co.nz

ISBN: 9781784980733 | Printed in India

Design by André Parker

# Contents

# Foreword

The suffering itself is bad enough—whether it is brought about by a physical condition or injury, by a sudden loss, or an ongoing situation—but what adds to our agony is our pursuit to discover some meaning in it. When our suffering seems random or senseless, and we can't come up with anything good to point to that has come out of it, the if-onlys are relentless. We don't want our suffering to be for nothing.

We can continue stewing in our chaotic thoughts and unanswered questions, or we can allow the perspective of the Scriptures to begin to shape our perspective. We can allow the truth of the Scriptures to correct our faulty assumptions about the "good" that God has promised to work all things together for. We can allow the hope of the Scriptures to diffuse our despair.

That's what Kristen and Sarah have provided in this solid book—a feast of perspective, truth, and hope to feed upon when our insides are eaten up with frustration, fear, disappointment, and difficulty. They have opened up and examined the Scriptures in search of wisdom and insight for themselves and for all who will invest themselves in this book.

In the midst of suffering, we often feel that there is nothing that can fix the hurt. And while Kristen and Sarah offer no quick or easy fixes (in other words, false promises) as they work their way through 2 Corinthians 4 and 5, what they do offer is very real and substantive:

~ encouragement that it is possible to suffer and "not lose heart"
~ the illumination of "the light of the knowledge of the glory of God in the face of Jesus Christ"

~ the privilege of exercising "the surpassing power" that "belongs to God and not to us"
~ the reality of being "afflicted," "perplexed," "persecuted," and "struck down" along with the rugged confidence that we are not "crushed," "despairing," "forsaken," or "destroyed"
~ the vibrancy of "the life of Jesus" being "manifested in our mortal flesh"
~ the experience of being renewed day by day
~ the expectation of an eternal weight of glory beyond all comparison

Because of what we read in 2 Corinthians 4 and 5, we have everything to look forward to, even when day-to-day life here is very hard— "a house not made with hands eternal in the heavens." And we're clear on what we should do even as we endure unwelcome and oftentimes unbearable suffering:

~ We are always of good courage.
~ We walk by faith, not by sight.
~ We make it our aim to please him.
~ We persuade others.
~ We are ambassadors for Christ.

Perhaps best of all in this passage that is so capably illuminated in this book, we discover the best news ever heard by anyone who has felt the impact of the curse on creation in their body or in their relationships or in their circumstances—the good news that the new creation has come. The new creation that will one day rid this world of the curse of sin and will heal all that is broken and disfigured and unwell has already begun its life-restoring, reconciling work. It's begun on the interior of our lives. All who are in Christ are even now drawing their life from his life, their health from his health, their thoughts from his thoughts, and their hope from him who is our hope. Even now he is making all things new.

As deeply and profoundly true as all that is presented in this book may be, anyone who has suffered knows that it is hard to receive instruction and encouragement from those whom we think have not suffered themselves. We want to hear from those who have walked, and perhaps continue to walk, in dark valleys, and yet have found Christ to be a light to them, the Spirit a comfort to them, the Father taking care of them. That's what makes Kristen and Sarah such good guides for those who hurt. May you find their companionship and insight a comfort to you on your own journey through the dark and difficult path of life in this world.

*Nancy Guthrie*
*Author of* What Grieving People Wish You Knew

Kristen is Ministry Content Manager at Unlocking the Bible and blogs at kristenwetherell.com. She is married to Brad.

 @KLWetherell

 kristen_wetherell

Sarah is married to Jeff and is mother to four young children. She lives in Chicago and blogs at setapart.net.

 @Swalts4

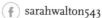 sarahwalton543

# Introduction

ife hurts. We're no strangers to this fact. It's why we wrote this book. And not simply because life hurts, but because there's hope even when it does.

We suspect that you're reading this because you're hurting, or because you love someone who is and wish that you could take away their pain. Perhaps the act of reading these pages is in itself a big deal for you because even the slightest effort feels like it drains you. No matter where you're coming from, whether you're suffering right now or not, we welcome you and are glad you're here.

And if you are currently suffering, we are sorry. We feel for you. But we will not say "we understand" because, most likely, we don't. We don't know your particular situation, or the years of struggle and darkness you've endured. Perhaps our stories share common threads, and if we were having coffee together, we might be so bold as to say, "Me too." Even though your suffering looks different than ours, and may be far greater and harder than we could imagine, we are walking through pain along with you. Pain of different sorts, but pain and suffering nonetheless.

When we are hurting, the pain affects our view of everything—including our view of God. Perhaps yours made you doubt God for the first time, or think about him for the first time. It may have made you grow in your love for him, or in your anger or disbelief. It may have caused you to pray for the first time, or the first time in a long time, or to stop praying at all. Most likely, it caused a conflicting set of feelings toward and questions about God. In all our pain, we have found hope in turning to him, not away from him, and in wrestling with reality rather than trying to ignore it. This book is in many ways a product of our journey and struggles.

In the following pages, you will find 30 biblical reflections to help you grasp God's purpose in your suffering. Each chapter is relatively short and accessible and (we hope) will take you to the truths of the Bible in a way that gives you hope. You will not find this book to be a comprehensive theology on suffering; nor will you find in it all the answers to your questions. You will find overlap and some repetition through the chapters, because God repeats great truths in his word, and we need reminding of them more than we may think! Though we dig deeply into God's word, this is not an exhaustive Bible study. We hope it will not only inform you intellectually, but help you emotionally.

And it was not written on the other side of suffering, but in the trenches and in the pain. There are moments when we marvel that we even finished this book at all, because of how our own sufferings were woven throughout the whole process.

## Kristen's Story

By junior year of college, the healthy, pain-free life I had known began to slowly disintegrate. Over a period of six years, I went from running races and performing theater and energetic days to perpetual weakness, inhibited movement, and chronic fatigue that put me in bed at 8:30pm. I moved to New York to pursue my dream of being a professional actor. And soon I moved back home again, exhausted and in pain. I knew something wasn't right, but no doctor could give me an answer. Every new visit left me with the question mark of defeat, as the easy answer would be repeated: "You're fine. You're young. Go home."

Yet, the problems worsened as the years passed. After a long day of typing at work, my arms and hands would ring with aching pain, to the point that I couldn't perform simple tasks like opening jars, doing laundry, even holding a pencil. My knees and feet raged with a similar pain, and my ability to exercise—even take short walks—vanished completely. The fatigue felt like waves of heaviness, like crawling through a dense fog, that would keep me from focus and any sense of normality. There were days when I wondered if my health was completely slipping away.

After six long years, my husband, Brad, and I saw a Lyme-literate doctor because my symptoms matched those of Lyme disease. The day the nurse called with confirmation was bittersweet: so good to have an answer; so scary to realize the road ahead of us. But by God's grace, and after two years of treatment, we have every reason to believe the Lyme is gone (I stay up later than Brad some nights!). Even still, as we sometimes say to people, "The war is won, but the city is ravaged." My body has been left weak and has years of rebuilding to do; some days are long and hard and strewn with discomfort. My struggle with pain looks different now, but it's still an everyday fight: discouragement stemming from dashed dreams, the frailty of a broken body, and the fight to persevere in hope.

## Sarah's Story

Without going into detail, during my four years of high school, I experienced bullying along with a form of abuse from peers. At the same time, circumstances that were out of my control brought some devastating re-direction in my life, the most difficult being the end of my athletic dreams. It all sent me into a downward spiral, leading to an eating disorder, a broken relationship with my parents, and depression that resulted in my being admitted to the hospital. It was there that I gave up my attempt to live both for Christ and for the world, and committed myself to following Christ.

Life seemed to become smoother for a time. I met my husband at 20, and to my great surprise I was married and a mother by 23. That was a decade or so ago—and the last 10 years have been greatly marked by loss. From a young age, our eldest son began displaying behavior that was defiant and destructive, and has caused a decade of confusion and chaos in our home. Countless doctors, tests, and evaluations seemed to leave doctors shaking their heads, and all we were left with in the end was an increased financial burden and growing fears. Everything was affected by his illness.

Along with that, my own health grew worse, and with each of the four children I bore, I found myself increasingly unable to function through my chronic pain and illness, along with an ankle injury that left me unable to do much of what I used to love. As my son's disorder continued to intensify, confusion and hurt began to grow in our other children, and our marriage began to suffer under the weight of it all. When we were at our lowest point, convinced that we couldn't endure anything else, my husband lost half of his income and we were forced to sell our dream home and downsize to a smaller rental home as medical expenses continued to pile up. Our family was in crisis. We were broken and wondering where God was and what he was doing. I found myself battling despair, hopelessness, and deep questions of faith that I had never had to face before.

In 2015 we were referred to a group of doctors who diagnosed me with Lyme disease. It wasn't long before this led to testing which revealed that the increasing illness in all four of our children, as well as my husband, were the result of Lyme disease being passed on from me. While we have clarity on one of the enemies we are fighting in our home, now we have a new battle before us: costly, time-consuming treatments, with continued confusion and no guaranteed certainty of complete healing. And then there is the loneliness—because my son's Lyme disease causes him to exhibit aggressive behavior, it keeps us from many normal parenting activities and leaves us feeling weary and broken by its multi-layered effects.

Every day is still a day of uncertainty as I endure the ups and downs of my son's challenges, all four children's Lyme disease, and my own chronic pain and fatigue. It is a moment-by-moment choice to press on through the trenches or give way to the crushing burden of my surrounding circumstances.

## Hope in Your Hurts

Suffering is an awful thing. In our hurt, we react in many ways: trying to hide ourselves from it, raging against it, melting down, attempting to numb the pain, even steeling our resolve to beat it. But there's more to suffering than merely getting through it with gritted teeth. Affliction invites us to wrestle with what God might be doing, to seek him right now in the midst of the pain. The wrestling doesn't come easily—but it does bring hope.

So we wrote this book for you, to point you to hope, because there's more to our suffering than meets the eye. This book is about the God who offers hope, even joy, in suffering. It's a journey through 2 Corinthians 4 and 5, where we see that God wants to give us hope not just beyond our hurts but in our hurts; that he wants us to see how he is able to work in and through suffering and ultimately give us himself.

If you are a Christian then—whether you feel it or not—these things are true of you and for you. If you are not, then they could be. Please remember as you read through that hope and joy in suffering are found in giving your life over to Jesus, to walk with him as your ruler and trust him as your rescuer.

You can read your way through the whole book, or go in any order; read one chapter a day when you have a moment, or one per week (though occasionally chapters refer to one another, we wrote them to work well in any order); go through it with a friend, a group, or by yourself; engage with the reflection questions at the end of each chapter and spend time in prayer; and write down your thoughts, insights, questions and prayers on the journaling pages. You can also use the other resources we've created for you at: thegoodbook.com/hopewhenithurts.

We praise God for how he has kindly allowed us to write this book, and we praise him that you are reading it. Our deep prayer is that you would be drawn closer to the suffering Savior, Jesus, who is also the risen, death-defeating Lord, able to give the most enduring hope there is.

*Blessed be the God and Father of our Lord Jesus Christ, the Father of mercies and God of all comfort, who comforts us in all our affliction, so that we may be able to comfort those who are in any affliction, with the comfort with which we ourselves are comforted by God.*

*(2 Corinthians 1 v 3-4)*

With love,

Kristen  Sarah

CHAPTER ONE

*Jesus Makes the Difference*

"God, who said, 'Let light shine out of darkness,'
has shone in our hearts to give the light of the knowledge
of the glory of God in the face of Jesus Christ"

2 CORINTHIANS 4 V 6

To suffer well, you will need Jesus.

Most likely you are reading this book because you or someone you care about is suffering, and you want to know how to get through it. You may be tired of self-help tactics, which never seem to work. You may well be wrestling with the hard questions of faith. You are fighting for joy in the pain, feeling confused about why God (if he is even there) would allow these trials to touch you.

You need a reminder of what is true, as you fight doubt and the depths of despair.

You want to know what it looks like to suffer well. Rest assured, friend—Sarah and I are with you. That is why we wrote this book.

As I have suffered over the last several years, these questions and many others have brought me to my knees (metaphorically-speaking—knee pain doesn't allow me to kneel). Suffering has made me desperate for truth, comfort, and peace. Through the searching and with God's help, I am grasping more and more that the gospel speaks into every aspect of my suffering, giving me hope and purpose.

This has come through a growing understanding of the gospel, and how it impacts every nook and cranny of life, from the mundane struggles to the most devastating of tragedies, as well as in the daily smiles and the greatest joys. As I write this, I'm laying on our couch, pain throbbing through my right leg. I'm not even sure how I managed this one—I hurt often for inexplicable reasons—but I'm acutely aware of pain's realness, and how it exposes my need.

And I need something to meet my need, something beyond meds and appointments and good luck. What I need, and you need, is the truth about Jesus Christ, because our suffering only makes any sense and we only retain any hope when we look at ourselves through a gospel lens.

Apart from the gospel, affliction is a dead end. It is the glass half-empty or worse. Suffering, when removed from a foundation of biblical truth, becomes an obstacle to "get through" at its best and, at its worst, brings us to a place of hopelessness and despair. Maybe that's where you are right now.

But the gospel offers hope, clarity, and joy in times that otherwise would be hopeless, confusing, and crushing. It sounds so simple! But there's a catch: to know this hope, clarity, and joy in suffering, we must know the true gospel. To soak in the light of it, we must think through the great salvation story of the Bible and preach it to ourselves on a daily basis. We need the gospel to suffer well, to bring God glory and to find our joy in him during the darkest of times.

Do you know the true gospel? If we sat down for coffee right now, would you be able to put it into words? And would those words make a practical difference in your every day life?

If your answer is no, you've no reason to worry! God's word provides all that we need for life and godliness, and here is what it says:

> The gospel is the stunning reality of what Jesus Christ has done for sinners—through his perfect life, his death on the cross, his death-defeating resurrection, and his heavenly ascension—to give us eternal life with him, out of his undeserved kindness. And our part is simply to say "yes" to his rescue and his rule.

The gospel is anything but normal; it is miraculous. We did nothing to deserve it; through it, we are given far more than we deserve.

In 2 Corinthians 4 v 3-6, the apostle Paul, the great missionary and church-planter, uses the metaphors of light and darkness to explain what Christ has done for us:

> *And even if our gospel is veiled, it is veiled to those who are perishing. In their case the god of this world has blinded the minds of the unbelievers, to keep them from seeing the light of the gospel of the glory of Christ, who is the image of God. For what we proclaim is not ourselves, but Jesus Christ as Lord, with ourselves as your servants for Jesus' sake. For God, who said, "Let light shine out of darkness," has shone in our hearts to give the light of the knowledge of the glory of God in the face of Jesus Christ.*

Light shining out of darkness—if you are a Christian, that's what happened when you believed! Jesus, the light of the world, caused his light and truth to dawn upon your heart, removing the veil and fog of unbelief that once blinded you to him. He gave the light; he did the shining, and you found you could see God for who he truly is and love the gospel for what it really is. And if you are reading this and you are not a Christian, I'm so glad and grateful you have picked this book up; this light is what you need to shine upon your heart.

So let's use Paul's explanation to discover what the gospel is and how the gospel enables us to suffer well:

## Suffering Is a Result of Sin Entering the World

God created us to know him, display him and be like him, to honor his loving authority and to follow him; he created us to walk in his light. But we each chose our own way, under our own authority, and rebelled against him. We chose the way of sin, and cast ourselves into spiritual darkness:

> *Although they knew God, they did not honor him as God or give thanks to him, but they became futile in their thinking, and their foolish hearts were darkened. (Romans 1 v 21)*

Our rebellion against God is the cause of our perishing in darkness. It has made us blind to enjoying life and light in God's presence—the gospel's declaration that Jesus is the God who made us and who knows what is best for us. Our blindness means that we are unable to see God's beauty, trust God's purposes, honor his authority, and dwell near to him—forever.

And sin not only affects humanity spiritually; it has also caused physical, mental, and environmental brokenness—suffering. It's the reason I'm laid up on this couch right now.

Now, I'm not in pain because I sinned. Suffering isn't always or necessarily a direct result of our own sin, but it is a direct result of sin's entrance into the world. It was Adam and Eve's rebellion against God in the Garden of Eden (Genesis 3) that ultimately caused physical and spiritual death, broken relationships, and the difficult, confusing, and tragic experiences we encounter every day.

This is, surprisingly, good news—though it may not feel like it! If suffering has no explanation—if it is merely the misalignment of some atoms, a case of bad luck in the face of a blind universe—then suffering can have no solution. But the general suffering of the human race is a consequence of the sinfulness of the human race. And the gospel is good news for sinners...

## Jesus Christ Saves Suffering Sinners

The darkness of sin left us needing the light of the Savior, and so he came. Through the gospel, God has shined his light into our hearts to see our need to be rescued from the darkness of sin—and Jesus is the one who does this for us!

Paul says that Jesus is the Christ, the promised King, who came to show us the wonder and nature of his eternal kingdom. He is also "Jesus" which means "God saves." This man took our place and took our sin, bore the darkness of hell that our sin deserves as he perished in our place, and rose again to open the way into his kingdom for those who would put their eternal trust in him. Because of Jesus, we can enjoy God's glory, light and power, rather than being scared of it, because in

Jesus we discover that there is a divine King against whom we have sinned—but we also find that the same King has died to forgive us.

So Jesus suffered to free our souls from eternal suffering. If God has opened your eyes to see your sin, and if you have trusted in Christ to save you from it, then sin no longer has the final word over the eternal destination of your soul—Jesus does. He became your suffering servant to keep you from perishing in sin. Jesus suffered death and was forsaken by his Father on the cross so that your death would become a gateway to eternal life.

Not only this, but Jesus suffered to comfort our hearts in our present sufferings. Through him, you are a child of God. You have a God who is near to you in your trials. You have a God who is at work to transform you into the image of Jesus, and who uses all things—even suffering—for your good.

## Suffering Will Come to an End

What God is doing in our souls will come to its climax when Jesus Christ returns to deal the final blow to death. Tears, mourning, and pain will be no more when he restores this creation to a new one and takes believers home to final glory (see Revelation 21 v 1-4), and the temporary reign of sin will end, as will all of its effects. "The light of the knowledge of the glory of God in the face of Jesus Christ" (2 Corinthians 4 v 6) will become perfectly clear to us, in all its dazzling wonder, as we finally meet our Lord and Savior face to face and worship him for eternity in the perfection of heaven.

The gospel tells you why suffering is. It tells you how suffering ends. Because of the light of Jesus Christ shining into our hearts, eternal darkness has been defeated, and our present darkness is being transformed.

We need God's gospel to suffer well. We need it every day, and never more than when life hurts. The better we know it, and the more we remind ourselves of it, the more precious we will realize it is. Without it, suffering makes no sense (and neither will this book!)—with it, suffering is transformed. Friend, this is only the beginning of our journey together—there is much more to come!—but it is the only place where we can start, and it will undergird everything else.

# Reflect

~ What do you hope to take away from this book as a whole? At the end of our time together, how do you hope to have changed?
~ Was any part of this chapter new for you? Do you struggle with any part of the gospel? If you have questions, I would encourage you to talk with a committed Christian or a pastor at a Bible-teaching church; and read through the book of Romans.
~ How do each of the three gospel insights on suffering speak to you in your particular trials? Take some time to think about—to meditate on—how the work of Christ speaks to your afflictions and hardships.

# Pray

*Heavenly Father, I am in awe of your gospel, and would like to be more so. I am a sinner in desperate need of salvation, and you have provided me a perfect Savior in Jesus Christ. Thank you for sparing me from your just punishment in him and for drawing near to me in him. Thank you that there is a life beyond pain and without tears. Please use this book to help me in my present suffering. Amen.*

*For further meditation:* Isaiah 53; Ephesians 1 v 3-10; Titus 2 v 11-14

# Journal

CHAPTER TWO

# His Power in Your Weakness

"But we have this treasure in jars of clay,
to show that the surpassing power belongs to
God and not to us"

2 CORINTHIANS 4 V 7

In some cultures, human weakness is not only looked down upon—it is resisted.

For instance, Americans will do almost anything to appear strong, capable, and worthy of admiration. We exercise our bodies with intensity, climb the corporate ladder at the expense of integrity, and struggle to accept the help of other people. Our society works by the principle that the way up is the road to success and value.

When we transfer this into our Christian faith, here is what happens: we believe that comfort is a right that Christ would never remove, and that success indicates a godly Christian life. This sense of entitlement has therefore deeply impacted the way Christians interpret and respond to suffering.

Think about how we talk about and react to a trial. We try to avoid it. We complain about it. We think we don't deserve it. We're embarrassed by it. We commiserate with others about it. We believe that God is mad at us, or just plain angry.

We hate weakness and will do almost anything to escape it.

One big problem with this approach is that weakness is real. Behind our masks, everyone is weak. It's inbuilt into our humanness in this world. We can't run from it, and thankfully we don't need to. What we need is a biblical understanding of the value of weakness (that's a strange-sounding phrase!), and how suffering is the tool God uses to expose it (that's another strange idea!).

Everything changes when we see weakness and suffering in the light of the gospel. For it is through human weakness that God's strength upholds us and is displayed to the world.

Here is the Bible's description of who a Christian is: "We [are those who] have this treasure in jars of clay." What treasure? The glorious gospel: the work of Jesus Christ to save sinners by grace through faith. And what is clay? A brittle, easily broken substance. And that's what I am. That's what you are. Paul is pointing out the frailty, disposability, and breakable nature of being human by using clay jars as his illustration.

He is saying two important things that we should take to heart. First, such a weak vessel is not fit to hold such a glorious treasure. Friends, you and I are jars of clay. On our own, we are sinners who are not fit to display the beautiful gospel of Christ, and our weaknesses only magnify this truth. Left to ourselves, we're not beautiful—we're sinners. Even after putting our trust in Jesus, we continue to have weakness in our physical bodies, as we struggle against aging, defects, declining health, and disease; and we also go on struggling against sin and failure.

Second, God has a purpose in placing such a treasure in such a jar. If we are not fit to hold such a glorious treasure as the gospel, then why in the world would God entrust it to us?! "To show that the surpassing power belongs to God and not to us." We are unfit, breakable, disposable vessels, and God has decided to use our weaknesses to display his power and love. A jar of clay might be cracked in a few places, making it unusable in the world's eyes, but God sees these deficiencies as a means to pour out and reveal more of himself.

The pastor Mark Dever hits the nail on the head when he says:

> When we rely on God, and God shows himself to be faithful, he gets the glory. This is what he has always intended. He does not intend for us to be strong, self-reliant, and without need of turning to him ... He intends

*for us to be weak and oppressed, and then to turn and rely on him,*
*because then he can provide what we need and thereby be glorified.*
*(The Message of the New Testament, page 203)*

Are you feeling weak today? Have your own deficiencies been exposed by suffering? Be comforted. You are a jar of clay, but you contain treasure, and your clay-ness serves to magnify the value of the treasure to you and to those around you.

Paul knew this from personal experience. The man who wrote the words we are listening to chapter by chapter in this book knew hurt, and had to cling to hope. He wrote from a prison cell, not from an ivory tower. Later in this letter to the church in Corinth, he talks of his thorn in the flesh, an ongoing affliction that exposed his clay-like weaknesses and caused him to depend fully on the strength of Christ:

*So to keep me from becoming conceited because of the surpassing great-*
*ness of the revelations, a thorn was given me in the flesh, a messenger of*
*Satan to harass me, to keep me from becoming conceited. Three times I*
*pleaded with the Lord about this, that it should leave me. But he said to*
*me, "My grace is sufficient for you, for my power is made perfect in weak-*
*ness." Therefore I will boast all the more gladly of my weaknesses, so that*
*the power of Christ may rest upon me. For the sake of Christ, then, I am*
*content with weaknesses, insults, hardships, persecutions, and calami-*
*ties. For when I am weak, then I am strong. (2 Corinthians 12 v 7-10)*

Through his experience as a jar of clay displaying the glorious treasure of the gospel, Paul teaches us how God's power is made perfect in our weakness.

## Exposing and Protecting

Weakness has the potential to bring out the worst in us. Pride is often what causes us to react negatively toward suffering. Because we like to appear in control and strong, we label anything that disrupts our plans and abilities as "bad" and "inconvenient."

Paul, however, understands that God is using his weakness to expose sin and protect him from pride. Hell is full of self-sufficient people who thought they needed no help. God will use your weakness to expose your sin, as he reveals to you how quickly your heart grasps at self-protection, convenience, comfort, and control. He will also use weakness to protect you from sin that results from having an easy life: pride, selfishness, greed, entitlement, laziness, complacency, and thanklessness, to name a few.

## Led to Depend on Him

When God exposes our sin and our frailty through our weakness, he doesn't leave us in despair—he leads us to Christ. Paul "pleaded with the Lord" about his thorn three times. Powerlessness drove him to prayer. And weakness drove him to consider what God's purpose might be.

When you feel weak, are you more concerned with having a pain-free life, or are you praying to the Lord in the midst of your pain? Do you wonder what God might be doing to help you spiritually, as well as asking him to help you with the pain?

Paul knows that God is able to remove the thorn if he wants to, but he trusts in the Lord's greater purpose. So he prays! Paul has a right view of God's purity and strength, so he approaches him humbly; and Paul knows that God loves him and is for him, so he approaches him confidently. You can do the same.

Your Father is near to you because of Christ Jesus. His presence and care are your comfort and strength. Let weakness drive you to depend on Christ, as you lay your requests before the Father with confidence that he hears your prayers and will ultimately do what is best for you.

## Showcasing His Strength

Here is a sentence that does not naturally come to my lips when my pain is at its worst:

> I am content with weaknesses, insults, hardships, persecutions, and calamities. (2 Corinthians 12 v 10)

How can Paul say that he is content in the face of all this pain? Many of us have our own versions of these hardships, which we often believe are anything but positive. It seems a stretch to say along with Paul that we are content!

But imagine being able to. Imagine if your contentment was out of the reach of your suffering. What is the key? Paul is content because he knows that God's strength will rest more fully upon him when he has nothing to give out of his own: "When I am weak, then I am strong." The defeat of Paul's self-sufficiency leads to the reign of God's power and strength within him. God-dependency is the path to true contentment.

Yes, we are jars of clay, and there are times and seasons of life where the clay is particularly cracked and dry. But always, we are jars of clay containing treasure—the treasure of the gospel. Rather than being downcast about our clay-ness, let's be awe-struck that we're treasure-bearers, and amazed that it's our very clay-ness that helps the treasure shine more brightly.

When God's power and strength reign in your weakness, you show the world—and you assure yourself—that you have hope beyond your present sufferings. You have opportunities that you would not otherwise have had to show the sufficiency of knowing Christ for your joy, and to share the salvation of Christ with those around you.

The world may tell us that weakness and suffering are evidences of failure, but we can know that they are a means to knowing and displaying the sufficient, perfect power of Christ. Knowing what we are, and knowing what we have, we become able to declare along with Paul, "I am content ... For when I am weak, then I am strong."

# Reflect

~ To what area of weakness do you need to apply the gospel today?
~ Who do you know that is going through a time of weakness, to whom you can give a reason for the hope that you have?
~ Have you considered that God's power reigns more fully in you when you are dependent on him? How might this change the way you pray? Take some time to meditate on this truth today, and thank him for how he redeems even your afflictions.

# Pray

*Almighty Father, your power is made perfect in my weakness. Help me not only to say this but to believe it. Help me not to run from or seek to hide my weakness. Help me instead to run to you in prayerful dependence. I need your help to apply the gospel to my hurts. Please enable me to find my contentment in your gospel and your strength, rather than in my circumstances, goodness, or abilities. Help me neither to resist my weakness out of pride, nor encourage others to do so. Please make me as weak as I must be to avoid pride, and as weak as I need to be to rely on Christ. Amen.*

*For further meditation:* Genesis 3 v 1-7; Job 42 v 1-6; John 9 v 1-12

# Journal

## CHAPTER THREE

*Affliction and Hardship*

"We are afflicted in every way,
but not crushed"

2 CORINTHIANS 4 V 8

If you are afflicted in every way—or even "merely" in *many* ways—how is it possible to live without being crushed by worry and anxiety?

I have often struggled in this area and if you have suffered or are suffering, I imagine you have too. A perpetual state of anxiety over what is ultimately out of our control comes to dominate our lives. Affliction causes anxiety—and anxiety crushes us as, bit by bit, it sucks the joy and peace from our lives.

In what ways do you feel anxious right now? Is it over your health, job, relationship status, finances, or family? Or is it a to-do list, a strained relationship, a difficult decision, or future unknowns causing the worry?

One of the greatest battles I wage on a daily basis is with anxiety over sickness, especially during the cold winter months when it's nearly impossible to avoid. After years of dealing with chronic pain and illness, I have become terrified and almost paralyzed with anxiety when someone in my home gets sick. The threat of catching an illness, in addition to the weariness of my daily discomforts, creates panic within my whole being.

The reality is that being a Christian doesn't exclude us from facing genuine fears and anxieties. Disease still strikes, friends still betray, bodies still fail, life still hurts. However, God has not given us a spirit of fear but of power and love and self-control (2 Timothy 1 v 7). Believers are equipped with the tools we need to fight this battle for peace. So what does it look like practically to find freedom in Christ from our anxieties and fears?

## Recognize the Root of Anxiety

*Therefore I tell you, do not be anxious about your life, what you will eat or what you will drink, nor about your body, what you will put on. Is not life more than food, and the body more than clothing? Look at the birds of the air: they neither sow nor reap nor gather into barns, and yet your heavenly Father feeds them. Are you not of more value than they? And which of you by being anxious can add a single hour to his span of life? (Matthew 6 v 25-27)*

These are Jesus' words. And Jesus tells us not to be anxious.

Isn't it helpful that Jesus offers questions for us to ponder as we address our anxious hearts? When we feel anxiety rise up within us, self-help tools and positive thinking will eventually fall short and leave us just as unsettled. We need to go directly to the root of our anxiety, which will often reveal a lack of trust in God's sovereignty, power, wisdom, or promises.

Not all anxiety stems from a lack of trust. There are sometimes physiological aspects involved in worry and these are not necessarily directly related to a spiritual matter in and of themselves. But what I am speaking of is the majority of us who struggle with the day-to-day anxieties of life and suffering. And oftentimes, those worries do stem from a lack of trust.

When panic sets in after one of my children comes home sick, I often become irritable, overwhelmed, and obsessive in my attempts to control my circumstances. I need to ask myself, "What is at the root of my anxiety in this moment?" The truth that I'd rather avoid is that I'm simply not willing to trust that Christ is in control over every aspect of my life—including germs, health, and physical pain. I'm actually choosing not to trust that God is good and will only allow what will be used for my ultimate good and to bring him glory. I'm deciding not to believe that Christ will equip me and provide what I need if my fears become reality. I'm allowing myself to fear pain more than I rest in God's love for me.

Put simply, I am choosing fear over trust. And that's the root of most of our worries. We are simply not convinced that God can come through for us or that he will come through for us.

## Remember What is Real

And in those moments, I need and you need to "consider" the reality about this world:

> And why are you anxious about clothing? Consider the lilies of the field, how they grow: they neither toil nor spin, yet I tell you, even Solomon in all his glory was not arrayed like one of these. But if God so clothes the grass of the field, which today is alive and tomorrow is thrown into the oven, will he not much more clothe you, O you of little faith? Therefore do not be anxious, saying, "What shall we eat?" or "What shall we drink?" or "What shall we wear?" For the Gentiles seek after all these things, and your heavenly Father knows that you need them all. (Matthew 6 v 28-32)

The truth is that God cares and that God provides. The evidence is all around us in nature. God knows what we need (which may be different than what we want, and that is when it is hard to trust). And God is, Jesus reminds us, the Father of his family. Fathers may withhold what is not good from their children, but they do not withhold what is needed by their children. A good father may not always explain himself to one of his children, but he will always be acting out of love for each of his children.

When I give in to anxieties, I am choosing to live as though this world is out of control, or under the control of an uncaring divine being. We need to consider reality. When we do that, we remember that this world is under the control of our Father, who cares for us more than we know.

# Cast Your Anxieties on Him

*Cast all your anxiety on him because he cares for you. (1 Peter 5 v 7, NIV)*

Because he cares, God wants to take your anxieties. And because he is God, his hands are big enough to hold what yours cannot. So we are told to "cast" our anxieties "on him." This is an intentional throwing off of what weighs us down onto God through prayer—a conscious effort, moment by moment, to live not by fear but by faith. He alone is our source of strength when our bodies give way; he alone is our source of hope when grief sends its crushing blow; he alone is our wisdom when we have limited vision and life-altering decisions to make; he alone is our rock when our earthly security is shaken.

# Believe God's Promises

*But seek first the kingdom of God and his righteousness, and all these things will be added to you. (Matthew 6 v 33)*

The greatest antidote to anxiety is to consistently remind ourselves of the unshakable promises we have in God's word. When a circumstance suddenly threatens our peace, we can be ready to push it back and cut it down with truth. Here are a few examples:

"I don't feel capable of accomplishing this task or responsibility. What if I don't do it right?"

*But he said to me, "My grace is sufficient for you, for my power is made perfect in weakness." Therefore I will boast all the more gladly of my weaknesses, so that the power of Christ may rest upon me.*

*(2 Corinthians 12 v 9)*

"I lost my job and am worried about how I will support my family."

*The Lord is at hand; do not be anxious about anything, but in every-thing by prayer and supplication with thanksgiving let your requests be*

*made known to God. And the peace of God, which surpasses all under-*
*standing, will guard your hearts and minds in Christ Jesus.*
*(Philippians 4 v 5-7)*

"I feel like I'm failing at being the parent that I know I should be. I'm trying to keep up with the demands, but I'm so weary and worried that I'm not doing enough."

*Come to me, all you who labor and are heavy laden, and I will give you rest. Take my yoke upon you, and learn from me, for I am gentle and lowly in heart, and you will find rest for your souls. For my yoke is easy, and my burden is light. (Matthew 11 v 28-30)*

"What if the very thing that I fear the most becomes a reality?"

*We know that in all things God works for the good of those who love Him, who have been called according to His purpose. (Romans 8 v 28)*

"If I don't meet someone soon, I may end up alone for the rest of my life."

*For he satisfies the longing soul, and the hungry soul he fills with good things. (Psalm 107 v 9)*

"I keep slipping back into the same pattern of sin and am worried that I will never be free from this struggle."

*But now that you have been set free from sin and have become slaves of God, the fruit you get leads to sanctification and its end, eternal life.*
*(Romans 6 v 22)*

"I don't know if this pain is worth enduring and I just want a way out."

*For this light momentary affliction is preparing for us an eternal weight of glory beyond all comparison, as we look not to the things that are seen but to the things that are unseen. For the things that are seen are transient, but the things that are unseen are eternal. (2 Corinthians 4 v 17-18)*

We do not have to live our lives anxiously toiling and striving to control the circumstances around us. Trust Christ, and know that every aspect of our lives is purposefully designed to make us more like him and bring glory to his name. After all, "He who did not spare his own Son but gave him up for us all, how will he not also with him graciously give us all things?" (Romans 8 v 32). There is, in reality, no need to fear. Not when you have such a Father.

# Reflect

~ What are you anxious about right now? Can you recognize an area of unbelief that your anxiety may be stemming from? Is there some desire to be in control that is driving that worry?

~ What would it look like to live by faith in your Father instead of worrying?

~ Which anxieties do you need to cast upon God right now?

# Pray

*Heavenly Father, it is easy to live a life plagued by anxiety and worry over my appearance, health, comforts, finances, responsibilities, relationships, and instability around the world. Oh, how quickly I forget what you have done for me and how you love me! Thank you that you have spoken directly to me in your word about how to deal with the anxieties and worries of life. Bring these truths to my mind when fear strikes and help me cast my anxieties on you with an unwavering faith when fear knocks on my door. Teach me to live courageously in your strength with the confident hope of eternity with you. Amen.*

*For further meditation:* Psalm 23 v 1-6; Isaiah 40 v 29-31; Philippians 4 v 6-7

Journal

_____

_____

_____

_____

_____

_____

_____

_____

_____

_____

_____

_____

_____

_____

_____

_____

_____

_____

_____

_____

_____

_____

_____

_____

_____

_____

CHAPTER FOUR

# When Feeling Crushed

"We are afflicted in every way,
but not crushed"

2 CORINTHIANS 4 V 8

Suffering can be so painful and dark that normalcy can seem like a distant memory from another life—an easier one, a happier one.

Like a dead weight bearing down upon our hearts, pain puts pressure on our faith and stirs up emotions that we find hard to confront or push back. "I don't know how much more of this I can handle," I've thought to myself. "Could my circumstances get any worse? I just want things to be normal again."

Even if we know the hope of the gospel and believe it with all of our hearts, we still feel this pressure. Pain and suffering were never meant to be a part of our everyday experience and so they feel wrong; but, because sin entered the world, it is part of normal life to feel, from time to time or all the time, "afflicted in every way," just as Paul described to the Corinthian church.

When Paul says "in every way," he means it. He was one hard-pressed man:

*Five times I received at the hands of the Jews the forty lashes less one. Three times I was beaten with rods. Once I was stoned. Three times I was shipwrecked; a night and a day I was adrift at sea; on frequent journeys, in danger from rivers, danger from robbers, danger from my own people, danger from Gentiles, danger in the city, danger in the wilderness, danger at sea, danger from false brothers; in toil and hardship, through many a sleepless night, in hunger and thirst, often without food, in cold and exposure. And, apart from other things, there is the daily pressure on me of my anxiety for all the churches.*

*(2 Corinthians 11 v 24-28)*

Danger. Exposure. Violence. Pressure. My guess is that you can resonate with Paul's words, not because you've gone through similar struggles but because of the overwhelming pressure of the struggles you have known. What affliction is threatening to crush you right now? What suffering is testing your faith?

Maybe you're fighting a malignant disease. Maybe it's a short-term illness that is keeping you from carrying out your plans. Or maybe you lost your job this week, and you're worried about feeding your family. Are you in the middle of a nasty relational feud? Or married to someone who is not following Christ?

Lyme disease threatens me. Because of Lyme and its ill effects, physical pain and weakness are my frequent visitors. There are times when, after an extended period of feeling well, stable, and hopeful, they rebound with a vengeance. I reach my limit during these regressions, as my faith feels pressed and my struggle to believe the gospel intensifies—and out pour the tears. I often cry because I'm angry, fearful, and worried. I wonder how much more I can take, if the struggle will ever end, and if any good will come of it.

I am tempted to believe that because I am afflicted in certain ways, I cannot get out of the downward spiral into being crushed in spirit as well as in body. How I long for my heart-cry in suffering to be like Paul's! How I long to believe this beautiful truth: I am afflicted in every way, but not crushed.

Oh, don't you want this? To have the confidence that the pressures of suffering will not defeat you?

# ✳ *Where to Look*

How can we learn to say along with Paul, "We are afflicted in every way, but not crushed"? We look to the cross, and to the One who was hanged on it.

> *Surely he has borne our griefs*
> *and carried our sorrows;*
> *yet we esteemed him stricken,*
> *smitten by God, and afflicted.*
> *But he was pierced for our transgressions;*
> *he was crushed for our iniquities... (Isaiah 53 v 4-5)*

Jesus, the perfect God-man, decided to drink the cup of suffering given to him by the Father. He was violently nailed to the cross by the Roman authorities. He was spat on, mocked, and hated by onlookers. As his lungs slowly failed him from crucifixion, he cried out, "My God, my God, why have you forsaken me?" Even God, with whom Jesus had enjoyed a perfect relationship from eternity past, had turned his face away.

And all because of our sin.

Jesus was pierced for our transgressions. He was crushed for our iniquities. He shouldered the burden of our sin upon his shoulders. Jesus willingly took the penalty of sin that we deserved, drinking the cup of spiritual death for us.

But this was not the end of the story:

> *Yet it was the will of the LORD to crush him;*
> *he has put him to grief;*
> *when his soul makes an offering for guilt,*
> *he shall see his offspring; he shall prolong his days;*
> *the will of the LORD shall prosper in his hand. (v 10)*

When Christ was nailed to the cross, God's will to save sinners was prospering. In drinking the cup of suffering, Jesus became the offering for our guilt, and his offering was joyfully accepted by God. This is why God raised him from the dead three days later; Jesus overcame death by willingly entering into it as the perfect sacrifice. In the words of the German pastor Dietrich Bonhoeffer, who died in a Nazi concentration camp during World War II, "Suffering is overcome by suffering, and becomes the way to communion with God" (*The Cost of Discipleship*, page 92).

God has taken our gravest affliction—death—and has overcome it in Christ, so that we would never be overcome by it. The Father crushed his Son so that we would never be crushed by sin and death, so that we would spend an eternity of joy in his presence.

## The Cross and Right Now

But what about right now? An eternity of joy with Christ awaits us, which is beyond amazing, but what about our present afflictions? What does the cross of Christ mean for the pressures laid on us today?

The cross means that God is not condemning us. If you have trusted Jesus, then he has been punished for your sin—all of it: past, present and future. You will never be eternally condemned by God. You can know that your trials are not expressions of God's anger, because all of it was poured out upon Jesus. There is no wrath left for those whose sins were borne on the cross.

So when you wonder if your affliction is God's way of getting back at you for something you've done, remember the cross. If you think you cannot come to God in worship and prayer when you experience pressure, remember the cross.

Yes, some afflictions are the natural consequence of our sinful choices, but the ultimate consequence has been nailed to the cross as Jesus bore our sins there, and God's purpose is never to punish his children, even when we sin against him. He may be disciplining us, so that we would see where we are in danger of running from him. But because of the cross, you can rest assured that God is not out to condemn you.

The cross means that God is for us and loves us—even when we cannot see what he is up to; even when we cannot see any purpose of discipline; even when suffering seems pointless. Because of the cross, we are free to view daily pressures through the lens of God's love and his work on our behalf. We know that God is for us, not against us, because he gave us Jesus.

The author and preacher Jared Wilson writes:

> *There is one great sign that you are loved more than you thought. It is the cross. And there is a still further sign that you will live in this love forever. It is the empty tomb. (The Wonder-Working God, page 59)*

The cross of Christ does not end in death, but leads to life! The resurrection of Jesus was the stamp of God's divine approval on his sacrifice.

Friend, Jesus Christ was crushed for you because the Father is for you and loves you. This gospel truth is your assurance and comfort when the pressures of suffering seem too great to bear. Surely the Son of God has borne your griefs and carried your sorrows. He was crushed so you would never be. Your afflictions are temporary because your sins have been dealt with. Your future is secure because he rose to life. You can say confidently along with Paul, "We are afflicted in every way, but not crushed."

## Reflect

~ How do your afflictions put you under pressure? In what ways do they cause you to feel burdened?

~ How does considering the sins for which Jesus was crushed put your present afflictions into perspective? How does knowing Jesus loves you that much change the way you see your current trials?

~ What is one way you can dwell on God's love for you today?

# Pray

*Lord Jesus, if you could take something as horrible as your death on the cross and use it for my salvation, how much more can you transform my present afflictions into eternal good. Thank you that what should utterly crush me has already crushed your Son. Give me courage to face my trials, give me confidence that you are loving me and not condemning me, and give me clarity to see how you might be disciplining me back to wholehearted devotion to you. And please enable me to remember that I am loved so deeply. Amen.*

*For further meditation:* Jeremiah 23 v 1-5; Luke 24 v 1-12; Colossians 1 v 15-20

# Journal

_____
_____
_____
_____
_____
_____
_____
_____
_____
_____
_____
_____
_____
_____
_____
_____
_____
_____
_____
_____
_____
_____
_____
_____
_____

CHAPTER FIVE

# Greater Than My Pain

"We are afflicted in every way,
but not crushed"

2 CORINTHIANS 4 V 8

Affliction has been a close, unwanted companion to me for the past several years. She is always near my side. She makes her presence known in many ways, and the truth that she will not crush me seems hard to grasp at times.

Pain is a powerful thing, often defeating self-confidence, mental strength, human resolve, and a positive attitude within moments. As I write this, with pain shooting through my body and my soul weary within me, I consider this great truth of 2 Corinthians. And some days, despite my greatest efforts to hold on to hope and strength, my soul and spirit grow weary in fighting through the physical pain I endure on a daily basis. I often find myself being led to a prayer of brokenness in these moments. "Oh Lord, what good am I to you in this place? How much more could I offer you if I were healthy, energized, and strong! Lord, what is the point of this pain?"

The reality is that physical or emotional pain, especially when it is chronic, has a way of stripping away the masks we tend to wear, leaving our hearts exposed and our self-sufficient ways of life threatened. It clears away the fog of empty distractions and suddenly makes us face the question: Is it worth following Jesus when this is what life will be like?

I love the words of Christina Rossetti, a 19th-century poet, in *A Better Resurrection*, portraying the raw effects of pain and heartache in this godly woman's life, as well as her choice to humbly surrender her will to the trustworthy hands of our Savior:

*I have no wit, no words, no tears;*
*My heart within me like a stone*
*Is numb'd too much for hopes or fears;*
*Look right, look left, I dwell alone;*
*I lift mine eyes, but dimm'd with grief*
*No everlasting hills I see;*
*My life is in the falling leaf:*
*O Jesus, quicken me.*

Though broken in body and weary in spirit, she clings to the one hope that remains. Her surrender is not a helpless, defeated surrender, but a desperate and humble cry of faith to lay down her desired life for more of the presence of Jesus. Is it really actually possible to think like this? How can I possibly feel this in my own pain and afflictions? How can you?

*For we do not have a high priest who is unable to sympathize with our weaknesses, but one who in every respect has been tempted as we are, yet without sin. Let us then with confidence draw near to the throne of grace, that we may receive mercy and find grace to help in time of need.*
*(Hebrews 4 v 15-16)*

Pain is never pleasant, but nothing can compare to the pain of eternity without God. And so my pain today is a small glimpse of what I have been saved from. How much more can we grasp the beautiful and glorious promise of eternity with our Savior, free from pain, when we have a daily reminder of what we have been saved from? This truth of the gospel gives us a reason, purpose and hope to endure.

I don't know about you, but I am quick to turn inward in my pain and feel as though no one can understand what I suffer; I am often tempted to grumble, mope, and pull away from those I love. But there is someone who understands—who has been through everything I am going through, and everything I will go through, and far, far more—Jesus.

So why do I often go to him last? The reality is that no one can fully enter into our pain in the way our Savior can, the only one who knows us intimately and has walked this hard road before us. We are not left to endure the pain of this life in loneliness and our own strength. Rather, we serve a God who bears the physical scars of his love for us, and sympathizes with us as one who has lived as a human being and suffered more than you or I will ever have to know. He longs to fill the broken pieces of our lives, often left by sin and suffering, with the hope of the gospel and the healing power of his presence. One thought about our afflictions can never be true—that no one understands them. We have a God with nail marks in his hands. We speak to a God whose time on earth was accompanied by the afflictions of poverty, of disappointment, of betrayal and mockery and beating and death.

And this Jesus offers us mercy and grace in our time of need. So cry out to him! God does not leave us to fend for ourselves. I'm so thankful for that! When we have nothing left and are struggling to put one foot in front of another, we can cry out to Jesus, who not only understands but strengthens us when we are weak, equips us when we are weary, and brings beauty out of our brokenness. Praise be to God that we have a hope beyond our pain because of the grace and mercy of Jesus Christ!

*My life is like a faded leaf,*
*My harvest dwindled to a husk:*
*Truly my life is void and brief*
*And tedious in the barren dusk;*
*My life is like a frozen thing,*
*No bud nor greenness can I see:*
*Yet rise it shall—the sap of Spring;*
*O Jesus, rise in me.*

As I write, I am speaking this truth to my own soul just as much as to yours. Though there are times when pain can seem almost unbearable, we have a hope that much of the suffering world does not know. While you naturally desire the healing of your body or your mind, Jesus desires the healing of your soul above all. And you will either allow the period of pain to bring you closer to Jesus, or to pull you away from Jesus. Be aware that the company of affliction can cause you to turn away from Jesus, in crippling bitterness or toward futile self-reliance; or it can cause you to turn to Jesus, trusting that he knows, cares and helps, and will one day bring you to a world where faith will become sight and pain will be no more.

So let's cry out to him in our pain! Although we are afflicted in every way, we will not be crushed because of the grace of Jesus Christ that is poured out to us. He will only allow what will be used for his good and loving purposes in your life and, if he has chosen to allow you to endure some form of pain or affliction, you can find strength in the promise that he will only allow for an allotted time what he intends to use for your good and his glory.

Don't give up or give way to despair, for there is a glorious treasure to be found when the pain of this world drives us to Jesus, and it is of far greater worth than any earthly relief. Yes, pain and affliction are real in this world. Jesus knows that. But what could crush you can, as you struggle on in faith, be the means of reshaping you.

*My life is like a broken bowl,*
*A broken bowl that cannot hold*
*One drop of water for my soul*
*Or cordial in the searching cold;*
*Cast in the fire the perish'd thing;*
*Melt and remold it, till it be*
*A royal cup for Him, my King:*
*O Jesus, drink of me.*

Affliction will be my close companion, it would seem, through this life. But when she tempts me to despair, I have a God who understands, and who helps, and who will use her to keep me his and mold me into his likeness. She will not defeat me, for he is greater than she, and will be loving me when she is gone.

# Reflect

~ Where do you turn when the pain in your life seems too much to bear?

~ Will you pour out everything you have to our Savior, trusting that he is powerful enough to speak into and bring glory out of even your greatest heartache and pain?

~ Are you willing to accept the pain in your life or a loved one's life as God's perfect will and purpose in this season?

~ Do you believe that Jesus can truly sympathize in all our weaknesses? Why or why not? If not, would you go to him in prayer, asking for him to meet you where you are and show you more of himself?

# Pray

*Oh Lord, there are times in this life when the pain seems too much to bear. We desire healing in this life and freedom from the bondage pain can bring, but we praise you that you have given us hope beyond our pain, joy beyond the heartache, and life beyond the death we deserve. Lord Jesus, forgive us for the bitterness and grumbling that pain can stir within us, and help us to know your saving power in a deeper way because of it. When we are weak, you are strong! By your grace, give us strength for today and hope for tomorrow. Thank you, Jesus, that though we are afflicted in every way, we are not crushed because of the hope of the gospel. May you be glorified in this pain and in our lives for the sake of your kingdom. Amen.*

*For further meditation:* Isaiah 53; Psalm 16

## Journal

CHAPTER SIX

# Peace Amid Confusion

"We are ... perplexed, but not driven
to despair"

2 CORINTHIANS 4 V 8

Have you experienced a time when it seemed as if God's hand was clearly leading you in a certain direction, when circumstances suddenly took an unexpected—and unpleasant—turn?

One of several such moments within my own family came a few years back when we were in a very heavy and scary place with our son and his behavioral problems. We were desperate for help and were seeking counsel and direction from people we trusted. After much prayer and receiving confirmation from several people regarding a certain doctor, we took steps to get into his highly sought-after practice. We were blown away when we were miraculously able to get an appointment the following week. Despite the high financial cost, we were so thankful that we finally seemed to be getting the help that we needed from a doctor we could trust.

It was only a few days after we had seen him that we discovered that the doctor was not the one we had thought we were seeing. He had taken the name of the practice after some kind of feud and was seeing patients who he knew thought they were seeing someone else.

Our excitement turned to shock and anger. Just as we were praising God for his clear guidance and provision, he allowed that very provision to be suddenly stripped away, leaving us perplexed and shaken.

Why had God not revealed this to us a week earlier, before we spent all that money and time? Why had God not protected us when we were seeking and trusting his direction?

God has a plan. But it is a plan that often looks perplexing from where I stand. And this kind of perplexing twist to life can make us angry and bitter. We're tempted to conclude that either God isn't really there, or that he is there and doesn't care—both of which lead us to despair.

But Paul doesn't despair—he is "perplexed" by what God is up to, and yet he is "not driven to despair." Why not?

*Faith is the assurance of things hoped for, the conviction of things not seen. (Hebrews 11 v 1)*

Circumstances that perplex us need not drive us to despair. Instead, they can take us to new depths of faith. They challenge us to trust solely in the promises of God, rather than creating a god of our own design in order to make sense of what perplexes us.

Yes, sometimes God gives us glimpses into his purposes, but the complexities of his ways are far beyond our ability to fully understand. The limited understanding we are given, however, can teach us not only to obey him but to trust him completely, whether we can make sense of God's purposes or not. As the theologian J.I. Packer said:

*This is the ultimate reason, from our stand-point, why God fills our lives with troubles and perplexities of one sort or another: it is to ensure that we shall learn to hold him fast. (Knowing God, page 227)*

After all, attempting to always make sense of God's mysterious purposes isn't actually faith. It's accepting only the parts of God that we are comfortable with or can explain to ourselves. If God is God and if you and I are not, then we can accept that our limited vision will see only a snapshot in time, while our sovereign Lord has created, upheld, sustained, purposefully determined, and worked through every moment from the beginning of time. Faith is not living a life without feeling perplexed; it is to live in trust while feeling perplexed.

So we need to unmask four misguided views that can contribute to the confusion and frustration we feel when God allows perplexing circumstances to unfold...

## A Short-Term View of Life

*And everyone who has left houses or brothers or sisters or father or mother or children or lands, for my name's sake, will receive a hundredfold and will inherit eternal life. (Matthew 19 v 29)*

My initial response to perplexing circumstances is naturally frustration, confusion, and at times, anger. Why? Because I am viewing my circumstances through a short-term lens, rather than an eternal one, and so I give more weight to how I feel in the moment and what I can make sense of than to the promises that God has given me in his word. He has promised to work for the good of those who love him. He has promised to lead them home. He has promised to give them an unspoiling, unimaginably wonderful inheritance. He has promised to weave their trials into the great, glorious story of what he is doing for his people and with his creation.

He has not promised it will all make sense right now.

Although we haven't been promised a road map for our lives, with all their twists and turns, we can trust the hand of God and learn to look at our circumstances from an eternal perspective. When circumstances perplex us, we can remain confident that every confusing turn of events, pointless inconvenience, tear that's shed, and sacrifice that's made is being divinely orchestrated for our good and to display God's glory until we meet him face to face.

## A Too-High View of Our Wisdom

We set ourselves up for disappointment and confusion when we attempt to make sense of each and every circumstance of our lives. We tend, as Westerners living in a technological age, to assume that we know what's best in the first place. When God does not follow our plans, he must be wrong, right? But...

*My thoughts are not your thoughts,*
  *neither are your ways my ways, declares the* LORD.
*For as the heavens are higher than the earth,*
  *so are my ways higher than your ways*
  *and my thoughts than your thoughts. (Isaiah 55 v 8-9)*

If God always acted in ways that made sense to us, then he certainly wouldn't have sent his sinless Son to die in our place, offering us complete forgiveness and acceptance freely through Christ before anyone even asked him to (Romans 5 v 8). The cross reminds us that although we cannot possibly make sense of all the ways of God, we can always find peace and reassurance in the detours of life because he has proved that in all his ways he is acting out of love.

## A No-Gospel View of God

When we can't make sense of our circumstances, we easily forget the truth that we are forgiven and loved by God, and view our trials as God punishing us (and their removal as God rewarding us) according to what we have done. This is to live by law, not gospel. So if something bad happens, we think, "I must have done something wrong." If something good happens, then I must have done something right. The answer therefore seems to be to work harder and be better.

The gospel says a different, better word to us in perplexity: God loves you as he loves his own Son. He is not punishing you because your punishment has already been served, on a wooden cross, by Another. So now...

*We know that for those who love God all things work together for good, for those who are called according to his purpose ... And those whom he predestined he also called, and those whom he called he also justified, and those whom he justified he also glorified. (Romans 8 v 28, 30)*

For those who love God—whether that love is great, small, or just clinging on—God works all things together for good. As we grasp this,

HOPE WHEN IT HURTS

we realize that the Lord won't waste a moment of the pain and suffering that often feels pointless and random to us. Living by law will crush you as you see your failures, or cause you to rage at God as you look at your goodness. Living out the gospel will give you stability, peace, and Someone to cling to, despite how circumstances may appear at the time.

## A Belief in God's Power but Not His Character

During my own little temper tantrums, I've said, "I believe God can, but I don't believe he will." I was not questioning his power to help, but his desire to. If he could help and didn't, then he wasn't loving me, was he?

But there is another answer. If God is powerful enough to change our circumstances but doesn't, it must mean he is determining them for reasons we cannot see at the time. Again, the cross tells me that all that he gives me is for my good—however it looks. Some circumstances we will never understand here on earth, but often we can look back and see God's faithful direction in the end.

## It's a Redirection

My husband has often said to me, "It's not a dead end; it's a redirection." After a season of several confusing redirections, we have sometimes been able to look back, praising God's faithfulness and saying in amazement, "Only God could have led us here." God's ways are higher than we can fully understand, but we can trust that he will always be faithful to his promises.

So why does God allow these confusing and troubling circumstances? To anchor us in Christ, by faith, and not in the false comfort of our circumstances or the foolish pride of our own wisdom. And this is why we do not despair. God knows what he is doing, even when we do not. God is directing all things according to his plan, even when it seems thoroughly perplexing to us. And his plan is good, and better than ours.

One of the most beautiful and Christ-glorifying pictures of faith is when a believer has no earthly evidence or confidence to fall back on except a wooden cross and an empty tomb, and yet trusts firmly in the loving sovereignty of Christ. Seemingly senseless and confusing circumstances give us opportunities to trust in and beautifully proclaim God's glory to a world searching for meaning in suffering.

When nothing seems to make sense in life and you feel yourself being tossed by the waves, you will not be driven onto the rocks of despair as you learn to anchor yourself with Christ's loving control, perfect wisdom, and unchanging character. Hold firm to the truth of the gospel and your anchor will not fail, and he will bring you into the harbor—however many redirections it requires.

## Reflect

~ Can you relate to one or more of these four mistakes that we are tempted to make in perplexing circumstances?
~ Where do you turn when circumstances don't make sense and seem out of line with how you think God would act?
~ Where in your life can you see God asking you to rest, wait, and trust in him, despite how circumstances may look?

## Pray

*Lord Jesus, you are worthy of being trusted in all areas of life, even when I am perplexed by circumstances in life. Help me to trust you because of who you are and not by what I can see and understand. Forgive the pride in my heart that leads me to trust in my own ways and doubt in yours. Increase my faith and use my trials to enable me to love you and your inscrutable ways more and more. Amen.*

*For further meditation:* Psalm 37 v 5; Psalm 118 v 8, Proverbs 3 v 5

# Journal

## CHAPTER SEVEN

# The Detours of Life

"We are ... perplexed, but not driven
to despair"

2 CORINTHIANS 4 V 8

*I* am not naturally gifted when it comes to "going with the flow."

A change of plans makes me sweat. I feel more relaxed and have more fun when people tell me what to expect of activities (even better, when I can plan them myself). My husband sees one of his main roles in our marriage as helping me loosen up, and he has succeeded! I'm learning to roll with change.

But what about a potentially life-altering change of plan, one that shifts the very foundations that we've built our dreams upon? That is much harder to "roll with." My guess is that you, like me, struggle with the major detours that confuse and dismantle the ideals we had etched out for our days.

The loss of a child. Health that has taken a turn for the worse. The sudden dismantling of a friendship. The destruction of personal property after a violent storm. The crumbling of our bodies. The list could go on.

Life's detours come in many different shapes and sizes, but all of them share one thing: we didn't see them coming. They catch us off-guard, leaving us frustrated, disoriented, even heartbroken. We question why things had to happen this way, at this time. Sooner or later, those questions are brought to God's door.

# Standing on the Shore

God's Old Testament people were no strangers to unexpected, inexplicable detours. God called them out from slavery in Egypt with remarkably little direction. Being commanded by God to pack up and move out of the land you've called home for centuries is hard enough (though leaving behind the harsh treatment of slavery was a welcome change). Being commanded by God to travel by a foolish route must have been even harder:

> When Pharaoh let the people go, God did not lead them by way of the land of the Philistines, although that was near. For God said, "Lest the people change their minds when they see war and return to Egypt." But God led the people around by the way of the wilderness toward the Red Sea ... And the LORD went before them by day in a pillar of cloud to lead them along the way, and by night in a pillar of fire to give them light, that they might travel by day and by night... (Exodus 13 v 17-18, 21)

Then God speaks in his inscrutable wisdom:

> And I will harden Pharaoh's heart, and he will pursue them, and I will get glory over Pharaoh and all his host, and the Egyptians shall know that I am the LORD. (14 v 4)

And so,

> When Pharaoh drew near, the people of Israel lifted up their eyes, and behold, the Egyptians were marching after them, and they feared greatly ... And Moses said to the people, "Fear not, stand firm, and see the salvation of the LORD, which he will work for you today. For the Egyptians whom you see today, you shall never see again. The LORD will fight for you, and you have only to be silent." ... And the people of Israel went into the midst of the sea on dry ground, the waters being a wall to them on their right hand and on their left. The Egyptians pursued and went in after them into the midst of the sea ... Thus the LORD saved Israel that day from the hand of the Egyptians, and Israel saw the Egyptians dead on the seashore. Israel saw the great power that the LORD used

*against the Egyptians, so the people feared the* LORD, *and they believed in the* LORD *and in his servant Moses. (14 v 10, 13-14, 22-23, 30-31)*

Then, standing on the eastern shore, the people praise the God who led them on this detour:

*You have led in your steadfast love the people whom you have redeemed; you have guided them by your strength to your holy abode. (15 v 13)*

God took the Israelites on a perplexing adventure: "God did not lead them by way of the land of the Philistines, although that was near." You can imagine the people thinking, *Wouldn't it be easier to take the direct route?* You probably cannot imagine the people's abject terror and despair as they stood with their backs to the sea and watched the Egyptian armies charge toward them. Their God-given detour had trapped them—yet the detour was not a mistake. It was a learning experience for them, and for us.

From this account, God gives several reasons to trust him in the perplexing, paradigm-shifting detours of life:

## God's Ways and Your Wisdom

The way God leads may not make sense to you, but his wisdom far exceeds your own. The Bible very purposefully records God's thoughts about the detour he chose for the Israelites: "Lest the people change their minds when they see war and return to Egypt." God knew something about his people that even they could not perceive about themselves.

And isn't this how it always is? God is our good Creator. He knit us together and perceives our thoughts from afar. Before a word is on our tongue, the Lord knows it. Nothing is hidden from his sight.

We, on the other hand, are limited in knowledge. We cannot know what is best for us because we are not the Creator, but a (small) part of his creation.

There is actually deep comfort in this humbling truth, because it tells you that there is One who sees and knows everything about you. As you come face to face with confusing, even painful, changes, you can trust that nothing is perplexing to God, that every change makes perfect sense to him, and that he can see both the beginning and the end.

## The Power of a God-Given Detour

The people "feared greatly" when they saw the Egyptians approaching. Again, imagine this scene. God's people think that they have finally been released from the nightmarish reality of slavery—only to find Pharaoh marching after them, seeing red and plotting revenge. Putting myself in their shoes, I can imagine the hot blood of fear and adrenaline pulsing through my veins, as my future of freedom disintegrates before my very eyes.

When the floor goes out from under you and you feel overwhelmed by your circumstances, how quickly do you succumb to fear? For me, it is very quickly—almost instantaneously. It doesn't take long for my weak faith to doubt God, while my "self-sufficiency responder mode" kicks into gear.

But when God literally piled the waters into heaps so his people could cross over the Red Sea to safety, "Israel saw the great power that the LORD used against the Egyptians, so the people feared the LORD." As God displays his endless power, the Israelites' fear is transformed. They no longer fear their enemies or their circumstances, but God, the stopper of the seas and the avenger of their adversaries. When God's detours teach us to stop relying on ourselves and what we can see, and start fearing the LORD and looking to him, they are detours of blessing.

I love this from Dietrich Bonhoeffer, the German theologian and pastor murdered by the Nazis in 1945: "Those who are still afraid of men have no fear of God, and those who have fear of God have ceased to be afraid of men" (*The Cost of Discipleship*, page 218). God displays his perfect power through paradigm-shifting detours so that we might fear him—and learn to trust him.

## Knowing God Through a Detour

"You have led in your steadfast love the people whom you have redeemed; you have guided them by your strength to your holy abode." This one verse contains a wealth of beautiful truth about who God is. If it were not for the Israelites' unexpected, perplexing Red Sea detour, they would not have known him in this way and would not have sung this song.

God demonstrates that his steadfast love is not tied to our understanding of his ways. He reveals that his work in bringing us home to be with him is not reliant upon our ability to trust him, but upon his sovereign plans. He proclaims that his power is made perfect in our weakness, and that his guidance through the swelling seas is not conditioned by our strength to endure the waves.

How could we rest in our eternal Comfort, unless he placed us in an uncomfortable season? How could we cling to our tender Shepherd, unless he exposed us to the elements of perplexing, hilly pastures? How could we take refuge in our strong Tower, unless he made the ground to shift beneath us?

## God's Detours Take You Home

The "holy abode" of God's presence will become real for you when you worship him face to face in glory. And how wonderful to think that you may do so standing next to someone who walked through the Red Sea?

*Therefore, since we are surrounded by so great a cloud of witnesses, let us also lay aside every weight, and sin which clings so closely, and let us run with endurance the race that is set before us, looking to Jesus, the founder and perfecter of our faith, who for the joy that was set before him endured the cross, despising the shame, and is seated at the right hand of the throne of God. (Hebrews 12 v 1-2)*

The believers who passed through the Red Sea are cheering us on as we navigate our own detours "with endurance." You will run the race marked out for you if you fix your eyes on Jesus rather than on the route.

One day, you will see why the "race ... set before" you was routed as it was. Today, you need only remember that Jesus knows more than you, loves you more than you know, calls for fear and trust from you... and that what you call detours, he calls the way home.

## Reflect

~ Think about a particular area of your life that feels perplexing. How does the truth that God is infinitely wise enable you to rest, even though you feel confused? Write out a prayer entrusting your confusion to his wisdom.

~ Ask God to help you identify any areas that you are attempting to control. Ask him to reign over your circumstances by his power, and to help you release control.

~ Reflect on some confusing times in your past that eventually God made clear to you. Praise him for his faithfulness, and entrust your present confusion to this same faithfulness.

## Pray

*Powerful and wise God, your ways are infinitely higher than mine, and your thoughts higher than my thoughts. I am in awe of your perfect wisdom, even when your purposes seem perplexing. I confess that I struggle to trust you when life doesn't go my way; I get angry and discouraged because I want control over my life. I praise you, for all your ways are righteous and good. Please use my detours to teach me what Israel learned at the Red Sea—to enable me to know you, fear you and trust you. Teach me about your character, root me more deeply in Christ, and display your glory through the detours of my life. Amen.*

*For further meditation:* Isaiah 55 v 6-9; Psalm 46

*Journal*

CHAPTER EIGHT

# God's Silence and Our Storms

"We are ... perplexed, but not
driven to despair"

2 CORINTHIANS 4 V 8

It had been over an hour. I stood there, holding the door shut to my son's room while he raged on the other side of it. His yet-to-be-diagnosed neurological disorder had been dominating our lives for years. My sometimes sweet, funny, determined little seven-year-old was experiencing a battle raging inside of him, and it was spilling out into every part of family life.

So there I stood, fighting against his surprising strength to get the door open. No matter what was on the agenda at this time, it all went out the window. My sole focus was our family's safety, as this illness turned my son into someone else. "How long will this one last?" I thought. An hour? Two? All I could do was try to hold back the tears that welled up in my eyes, pray... and wait.

On days when I feel the crushing weight of my son's special needs while trying to care for three other children, along with my own struggling health, I cry out to the Lord, "Where are you in all this pain? I just don't know if I can do this anymore."

Why does it sometimes seem as if God is silent in the midst of the storms that threaten our lives? If you're reading this, it's likely because life didn't map out as you'd wanted it to. And so, like me, you may know what it is to ask, or maybe even to scream: "Jesus, where are you in this storm? Don't you care?!"

As I wrestled with my own unsettling emotions of being perplexed by what God was allowing in both my son and my family's life, the Holy Spirit drew me to a familiar passage in Matthew:

> *And when he got into the boat, his disciples followed him. And behold, there arose a great storm on the sea, so that the boat was being swamped by the waves; but he was asleep. And they went and woke him, saying, "Save us, Lord; we are perishing." And he said to them, "Why are you afraid, O you of little faith?" Then he rose and rebuked the winds and the sea, and there was a great calm. And the men marveled, saying, "What sort of man is this, that even winds and sea obey him?" (Matthew 8 v 23-27)*

I can relate to this. Of course, I've never been on a boat with a sleeping Jesus. But I know how it feels to think that he was asleep as the storms raged around me. And it's often in these moments that we struggle to see and think clearly, as our emotions blur the lens of truth. The middle of a storm is, after all, the worst place to think clearly and respond wisely. So it's wonderful that here, we have the privilege of watching this particular real storm unfold from an outsider's perspective. We are able to stand back and glean from the lessons the disciples learned, rather than listening to our own emotions, excusing our own reactions, and drawing possibly misguided conclusions.

So, what had the disciples learned by the time they arrived, soaking wet but amazingly alive, on the other side of the sea? What are we to learn?

## Led into the Storm

Jesus sometimes leads us to places that contain deep struggle, but he takes us there to reveal that his power is greater than any storm that may brew. While we may not desire the storm itself, or may even fear it, we can trust that God will not lead us anywhere that will not ultimately kindle or rekindle our faith. In fact, the very storms that he allows us to endure are proof of his grace and love for us, as they bring us into a deeper reliance upon him.

## Following into the Storm

If we have chosen to follow Christ, we must understand that following him will include storms and suffering. Jesus says:

> If anyone would come after me, let him deny himself and take up his cross daily and follow me. For whoever would save his life will lose it, but whoever loses his life for my sake will save it. (Luke 9 v 23-24)

We can't pick and choose when it comes to following Christ. Either we follow him, or we don't. We can't choose blessing and not suffering. For suffering seems to be where some of the greatest blessings are found, just as the blessing of our salvation is the product of Christ's painful suffering on the cross. Obedience will sometimes take us into suffering—and, while it's good and right to seek out God-honoring ways to ease our suffering, we must be careful that we are not so determined to find a short cut through our struggles that we miss what God intends to do in and through them.

## Sleeping in the Storm

Does God sometimes seem to be asleep in your storm? He does to me. But that doesn't make him less God or less present. Though Jesus slept as a man, he was still fully God and in control. He went to "sleep" to accomplish his purposes in growing the disciples' faith, not to abandon them. If God seems to be silent through your many prayers and pleas for answers, be encouraged and assured that he is still present and faithfully working to accomplish his purposes in our own hearts as he is in our circumstances. His silence never speaks of a lack of love or attention.

# Don't Row Harder... Cry Out

So often, when trouble enters our lives, we try to fix it in our own strength and limited understanding, rather than crying out to the One who has all the strength. Then, when our attempts fail or circumstances don't change according to our timetable, we get frustrated and anxious instead of trusting that Jesus will bring about what is best for us in his own, perfect timetable.

Sometimes, we need to stop rowing and start crying out. Problems we can't fix are opportunities to recognize the truth—we can't do life on our own, and we certainly can't do death on our own. Choose to cry out to him, question him even, and then trust him and wait on him. Learn to wait on him in faith rather than working hard in self-reliance.

Jesus asked, "Why are you afraid, O you of little faith"?

The disciples were afraid because their faith was based on what they could see and understand, instead of being based on the truth that Jesus was God. Right now in my life, I see no end to the suffering. No one can or should promise me that it will all be "okay" and that God will choose to heal our son and the rest of our family, or that he will ease the pain surrounding our life. However, God tells us not to be afraid, even when we don't see any hope in our immediate circumstances. Why? Because he is God, and even the winds and the sea obey him. And he will only let the storm rage as long as he knows it is necessary for our good and for his glory to be revealed. I do not know how God will help, or when he will put a stop to it. But I know he is at work, and knows best. I have no need to be afraid. Neither do you.

# Jesus Calms Storms

Despite his followers' "little faith," Jesus still acted. He calmed the storm and saved their lives—but not until they had seen their lack of and need for a Savior. Do we try to do all the right things, thinking that God will see our efforts and calm our storm? Do we try to pull up our boot straps to prove that we are "strong" and in control of our lives? Or do we humbly admit our dependence on Christ and cry out to him to rescue us from the storms from which we are helpless to save ourselves?

Trials may leave us perplexed, but they need never leave us hopeless. Why? Because as we acknowledge and accept our own inability to understand all of the unsearchable ways of God, we learn to wait, rest, and rely solely on his power and promises to be revealed. And we learn to look forward to the day when he will say to our storms, *Enough. Be still.* No, it may not be as quickly as we'd like, and it may not be until the day we meet him face to face, but nonetheless, he will do it. So, perplexed as we are in the midst of the storm, we don't despair because we know there will be an end to the storm.

One day, whether it be in my lifetime or eternity to come, the pain, fear, and weariness over my son will end. In his timing (not mine), Christ will say *Enough* to the suffering in my life, and will calm the storms raging around me. I don't know how he will write the rest of my story or what the future holds for my son and our family, but I am confident that Christ will carry me through until the day he commands the water and the waves to "be still."

So whatever storm you are facing... cling to him! Cry out to him! Then wait, watch, and anticipate. The greater the storm, the greater the opportunity for you to rely on Jesus, and the greater the joy and the awe you will experience when his glory and power are shown through it.

## Reflect

~ Have you experienced a trial during which God seemed to be silent, leaving you perplexed and questioning God's ways? Did it cause you to go your own way and row harder, or did it turn you to the Lord in greater reliance? Why did you respond that way, do you think?

~ If you are in the middle of a storm right now, what have you learned from looking at the Lord and his disciples in this sea-storm? How do you need it to encourage you or reshape your reaction?

~ How does it make you feel to know that, if you cling to him, one day Christ will say, *Enough. Be still?*

# *Pray*

*Lord Jesus, at times, grief, heartache, and pain can feel so crippling that it's hard to keep my eyes fixed on you. Oh Lord, I cannot and do not want to go through this life without you, but at times it feels as though you are silent in the storms around me. Thank you that even when I am perplexed by the circumstances of my life, you are still present, still in control, and still God. Help me to resist the temptation to rely on myself, and give me greater reliance on you now, and greater joy at the prospect of you calming my storms. Help me cling to that truth as I seek to trust you more through the storms of life. Amen.*

*For further meditation:* Psalm 37 v 3-5; Hebrews 10:23; Hebrews 11 v 1; Psalm 91 v 4

# Journal

CHAPTER NINE

# The Not-Surprise of Persecution

"We are ... persecuted, but not forsaken"

2 CORINTHIANS 4 V 8-9

For the last few centuries, the persecution of Christians has been a distant concept for those of us in the West. We have been protected from most of the atrocities and fears that many believers face around the world every day. For many today, as for Paul in his day, to choose Christ is not merely a sacrifice of worldly dreams and pursuits; it is a choice to risk livelihood, loved ones, and life.

But persecution is coming closer for those of us who have never really had to choose between comfort and Christ. Although nothing like that in Syria, Afghanistan, northern Nigeria, and much of the world, persecution of Christians in the West is real and growing. When we think about trials and talk about sufferings, we must never do so without considering those that come simply and only as a result of belonging to Christ.

And most of us are not prepared for this. So we tend to see it as a disaster, and one to be avoided if and where we can. We need to view Christian suffering in a Christian way—and here Paul gives us the perspective to have on persecution, in order that, when it comes, we would remain steadfast and patient in the face of it. His message is simple: we may be persecuted, but we cannot be forsaken. Whatever level of persecution we face—whether we lose a friend or a promotion or we lose our home or our life—we need to understand and be confident in this perspective.

*Persecuted, but never forsaken.* That's the promise that James unpacks in more detail as he writes to believers who are suffering because they are believers. What he tells them, we need to hear.

## Flourishing and Forever

*Come now, you rich, weep and howl ... You have laid up treasure in the last days. Behold, the wages of the laborers who mowed your fields, which you kept back by fraud, are crying out against you, and the cries of the harvesters have reached the ears of the Lord of hosts. You have lived on the earth in luxury and in self-indulgence. You have fattened your hearts in a day of slaughter. You have condemned and murdered the righteous person. He does not resist you ... Do not grumble against one another, brothers, so that you may not be judged; behold, the Judge is standing at the door.*

*(James 5 v 1, 3b-6, 9)*

Not only were the Christians James was writing to being oppressed and robbed of wages they had earned, but they were watching the wealthy flourish in evil, luxury and self-indulgence.

Doesn't this often seem true for us as well? The persecutor—the mocker and the exploiter—often seems to flourish and succeed, even at the believer's expense. But don't be fooled into forgetting the future. James speaks directly to the persecutors: "You have lived on the earth in luxury and in self-indulgence. You have fattened your hearts in a day of slaughter" (v 5). These rich persecutors were given over to their self-indulgence and were blind to the day of judgment. The only reward for being a persecutor is eternal judgment at the hand of God.

Short-term prosperity and self-protection are never worth the cost of our eternal life—the present must always be seen in light of the future. Judgment is coming, so hold fast to what is lasting and hold on to Christ.

## Persecution and Forever

*Be patient, therefore, brothers, until the coming of the Lord. See how the farmer waits for the precious fruit of the earth, being patient about it, until it receives the early and the late rains. You also, be patient. Establish your hearts, for the coming of the Lord is at hand.*
*(James 5 v 7-8)*

Just as the farmer waits for the precious fruit of the earth, we wait for the glorious return of Jesus Christ. We do not suffer in persecution as those without hope—we can remain patient, confident that the day is coming when the Lord will return in all his glory to rescue his children. We may be persecuted, but we are never forsaken. Judgment and salvation are "at hand" and persecution prevents neither, however it may look and however we might feel—in fact, it makes both more precious to us. So "be patient." Don't give up. Don't take revenge. Judgment and salvation are coming closer.

## Blessing and Persecution Are Not Opposites

*As an example of suffering and patience, brothers, take the prophets who spoke in the name of the Lord. Behold, we consider those blessed who remained steadfast. (James 5 v 10-11)*

My last two years of high school were a time of heartache, anger and confusion. I had been an athlete all of my life and had my eyes set on a college scholarship for basketball. I also wanted to experience an overseas mission trip, so I committed to go on one. And then I discovered that it clashed with the varsity state basketball tournament.

I went on the missions trip, and it was wonderful. But I paid dearly for it the following year. Not only had I given up the prestige of winning the state title, but my basketball coach suddenly became hostile toward me. He refused to let me play, verbally abused me on the basketball court and behind closed doors, and made it clear that he was angry with me for my choice to choose the missions trip over the basketball. It cost me my scholarship.

And for a while I wondered, "Was it worth it—to give up that tournament and that scholarship and experience this persecution?"

However, as I reflect on this experience, the cost of following Christ, which seemed so high at the time, was actually a purchase of blessing. I discovered more of how precious Christ is and how joyful it is to follow him wholeheartedly. I had assumed that persecution could not bring blessing, but would only rob me of it. I found that in fact they are not opposites, but partners.

Of course, my persecution is almost embarrassingly minor in comparison to the persecution being experienced around the globe. But I'm confident my point still stands, because I see it in James as well as on my basketball court.

The prophets were people greatly blessed. They heard from God and spoke for God. Their names are still spoken of today. They got to see glimmers of Christ's coming centuries before. And yet the prophets were also people greatly persecuted. They were richly blessed and eternally rewarded because they knew what it was like to walk closely and intimately with the Lord despite earthly pain, sorrow, and persecution. Their confidence could not be shaken because their reward was an eternal one.

If we think that suffering and blessing can't co-exist, we will always be seeking shallow pleasures and comforts, and we will miss out on the deep blessings of walking closely with Christ in suffering. The world to come means that we can be pained and privileged at the same time.

 ## Perspective and Prayer

*Is anyone among you suffering? Let him pray. (James 5 v 13)*

The pastor and theologian John MacArthur writes:

> *The antidote to suffering caused by evil treatment or persecution is seeking God's comfort through prayer.*
> *(James: Guidelines for a Happy Life, page 94)*

So are you afflicted? Pray! Are you enduring persecution in your job, family, or ministry? Pray! Are things going well for you right now and you are afraid to lose your comfort? Pray! In good times and bad, we need to draw near to the Lord in prayer. It will not only draw us into a greater intimacy with Christ, but it will bring the comfort we need to face the fear and pain of suffering and persecution.

## Hands Full of Treasures

Betty Scott Stam followed the call of Christ in the early 1900's to do missions work in China, and was married soon after she arrived. Just months after giving birth to their only child, she and her husband were arrested by Communist soldiers. Betty, knowing she was going to her death, hid her daughter before being led to her execution, allowing fellow Christians to bring the girl to safety. That following day, Betty and her husband were beheaded.

Betty gave up her home, earthly security, and comforts. She lost the chance to grow old with her husband, to raise her only daughter, and to experience all the opportunities that this life offers. From the outside, her life looks wasted, her decisions misguided, and her God very distant. But that wasn't Betty's view. Here is what she prayed and what she said:

> Lord, I give up all my own purposes and plans, all my own desires and hopes and ambitions, and accept Thy will for my life. I give myself, my life, my all utterly to Thee, to be Thine forever. I hand over to Thy keeping all my friendships; all the people whom I love are to take a second place in my heart. Fill me and seal me with Thy Holy Spirit. Work out Thy whole will in my life, at any cost, now and forever.

> When we consecrate ourselves to God, we think we are making a great sacrifice, and doing lots for Him, when really we are only letting go some little, bitsie trinkets we have been grabbing, and when our hands are empty, He fills them full of His treasures.
> (Taken from The Triumph of John and Betty Stam
> by Mrs Howard Taylor, page 35)

She was persecuted, but she knew she was not forsaken. And neither are we. Because we have Christ, our hands are full of treasures, and they will be for all of eternity.

## Reflect

~ What is your instinctive view of persecution for being a Christian? To what extent is that shaped by your culture, your upbringing, your experience of life so far, and your reading of God's word?

~ Have you experienced in your life, or seen in someone else's, how blessing and persecution can go hand in hand? How does this shape your view of suffering for following Christ?

~ Do you love comfort or Christ? How does this show itself in your life?

## Pray

*Heavenly Father, it grieves my heart to think of brothers and sisters around the world being persecuted and martyred for proclaiming their faith in you. Help them to remember the future, and to know that judgment and salvation are on their way. Enable them to walk forward into trials with faith in you and love for their oppressors. And make me willing to suffer for Christ instead of worshiping comfort. Whatever else I may suffer or face, grant me the courage to stand firm for Christ even when that costs me. Amen.*

*For further meditation:* 2 Corinthians 12 v 10; Romans 8 v 35-36; 2 Thessalonians 1 v 4

## Journal

_____
_____
_____
_____
_____
_____
_____
_____
_____
_____
_____
_____
_____
_____
_____
_____
_____
_____
_____
_____
_____
_____
_____
_____
_____

CHAPTER TEN

# The Opportunity of Your Suffering

"We are ... persecuted, but not forsaken"

2 CORINTHIANS 4 V 8-9

Picture someone you know well who is not a Christian. As they watch you walk through suffering, what do they see? What do they hear coming from your lips? What are you communicating to them about the hope that you have?

Suffering can be distracting. It has the potential to embitter the spirit, harden the heart, and paralyze the will. Turning us inward, suffering often keeps us from seeing opportunities that God is placing around us to love others and share the gospel with them. At times, we are tempted to set aside proclaiming the gospel because we are defeated by sin, exhausted from bodily pain, or emotionally spent from attempts to reconcile broken relationships. Suffering seems to require all of our attention and effort as it drains us of resources. We feel we have nothing left to give. We just want to get through it, and that is enough of a challenge, without adding to it.

Remember that we are "jars of clay" (v 7). Those cracks exist for a purpose: to shine forth the great light of the gospel, which is our treasured possession, even in suffering. Especially then. It is the light of this wonderful truth that is ours to display and proclaim through our unique "cracks," and what an opportunity this is.

While chained in a Roman prison, Paul wrote a letter to the Colossian Christians. One of his closing statements is this:

*Continue steadfastly in prayer, being watchful in it with thanksgiving. At the same time, pray also for us, that God may open to us a door for the word, to declare the mystery of Christ, on account of which I am in prison—that I may make it clear, which is how I ought to speak. Walk in wisdom toward outsiders, making the best use of the time. Let your speech always be gracious, seasoned with salt, so that you may know how you ought to answer each person. (Colossians 4 v 2-6)*

Notice where Paul is as he writes about proclaiming the gospel—in prison. He is suffering; yet it seems that he is increasingly empowered by his situation, not defeated by it. Paul's physical chains have encouraged him to keep proclaiming the truth that has spiritually unchained and freed him! More than this, Paul asks for prayer from the church in Colossae, that his team may pour forth the light of Christ through the "cracks" of their imprisonment, which they received for being faithful gospel-proclaimers in the first place.

In prison, yet empowered. In prison, yet proclaiming truth. In prison, yet prayerful. Persecuted, yet not forsaken—instead, witnessing. This is not an embittered, hardened, paralyzed man. He is not distracted. No, this servant of Christ knew that his "cracks" and his persecutions were opportunities for gospel outpouring, not obstacles to be papered over or ignored. In Christ's light, suffering is a ministry, not a millstone. It is a gift, not a glitch in the plan.

Can you see your suffering as giving you a unique opportunity to proclaim the mystery of Christ clearly to unbelievers? Whether they are persecutors who hate you, or outsiders who are curious about Christ, these people need the hope that you have. Picture again the person you envisioned earlier. They are an important part of the ministry of suffering that God has entrusted to you. They are watching you, and they are listening to you. What are they seeing, and what are they hearing?

## People Are Watching

"Walk in wisdom toward outsiders, making the best use of the time." What does it look like for a suffering Christian to walk in wisdom around outsiders? What unique opportunity does our suffering give us? Unbelievers are watching how we suffer. They are looking to see how we handle the lot that God gives us. They are answering the basic questions of hope: "How is this person able to endure? How well can their belief system bear the pressure of an unasked-for turn? Does their joy survive in suffering?"

When life is going well, Christian joy and worldly happiness are hard to distinguish from each other. But when life is falling apart, and worldly happiness has long since fled, Christian joy can shine forth clearly and uniquely. Since the world sees suffering as a negative thing, we have an enormous opportunity to catch people off-guard and make them question their understanding of affliction, as well as how a person is able to persevere through it.

But how is this joy produced?

Paul says that the first key to displaying the gospel through our actions is watchful, thankful prayer. Any display of the truth to others starts at the feet of Jesus. We cannot give to others what we do not possess ourselves! So we draw near to God in prayer because needing him is our natural state, and knowing him and serving him is our greatest delight and reward.

Read this description of one gospel preacher's experience of watchful, thankful prayer from the Second Great Awakening in the early 1800's, when millions across the US turned to Christ: "Now, if ever, I enjoyed communion with God. He shone sweetly upon me, and I reflected back his beams in fervent, admiring, adoring love." The natural result of spending time before the throne of grace is an ability to reflect the One who reigns upon it. How might your joy in the gospel cause outsiders to wonder about their own uncertain, worldly happiness? What would it look like to display the fervent, admiring, adoring love of God to them in our suffering?

## People Are Listening

The second key to displaying the gospel involves entering into conversation with people. Though your actions may demonstrate God's work in your heart, by themselves they are not sufficient for sharing the whole gospel of Christ. So we speak of the crucified and risen Jesus with our words.

It is grace-filled, clear conversation that proclaims our answer to the world's question of hope. "Let your speech always be gracious, seasoned with salt, so that you may know how you ought to answer each person." You may have no better platform from which to proclaim God's grace in the gospel than that of your own suffering. Your conversations about struggles and pain can be surprisingly full of grace—talking about God's grace and speaking with grace to others. Your conversations can also be full of salt, full of interest in other people—not focused entirely and only on your suffering. Salty conversation raises questions, and then you can answer people in ways that point to God's goodness and, supremely, the gospel.

It is in answering everyone with truth and love, whether that is our unsaved neighbors or our hostile persecutors, that we make the most of every opportunity to proclaim that our God will never leave or forsake those who are in Christ, especially in times of suffering.

## The Light Pours Through the Cracks

As I write this, my husband, sister, and I are excitedly awaiting our parent's surprise 30th anniversary party. The plans have been months in the making, and the guest list is set. Tonight, a big group of their friends will gather at their home, and I imagine we will have many conversations about work, marriage, family, and health. So I've been thinking this morning, "What will I say if they ask how I've been feeling lately? What hope will I communicate to them?"

I could pretend everything is fine. Or I could act as though I'm completely discouraged. I could talk about improvements in my health in a completely secular way, of doctors and diagnoses; or I could talk about them as gifts from God. I could talk about areas of regression as devastating setbacks, or as strangely-wrapped gifts from his hand. Christ has set me free from the chains of a self-focused, sin-bound life, even when the physical chains of suffering are very real. He has entrusted me with the mystery of the gospel, and he intends for it to pour through my "cracks" as my life and my words proclaim him to those around me.

What about you? What unique opportunities to proclaim Christ clearly has God entrusted to you? By his grace, your suffering is a ministry—the light of the gospel pouring through the "cracks" of your affliction and into the heads and hearts of those around you. The way you suffer speaks volumes, and it tells a story. Let it speak loudly of the gospel of hope when it hurts, and of the God who brought hope through his sufferings.

## Reflect

~ Take an honest look at your response to suffering. Do your actions and words proclaim Christ's salvation and sufficiency to others? If not, and they know you are a Christian, what are you inadvertently teaching them about Christian faith?

~ What could you spend time giving thanks for in prayer today? How might you form a habit of thanksgiving?

~ If you had an opportunity to talk about your suffering in a way that shared the gospel today, what would you say? You could even write down some thoughts so you are watchful and prepared.

## Pray

*Almighty God, thank you for sending your Son so that I might proclaim him to others! Draw me to you through watchful, thankful prayer. Make my actions worthy of your gospel, and show me who I might talk to about you, and who I might listen to. Give me words that are grace-filled, wise, and timely. Help me to see how my trials can be cracks through which you can show yourself. Please save those around me through my witness in the pain. Give me strength not to give up or shut down, but to display the treasure of the gospel, for your sake. Amen.*

*For further meditation:* Matthew 10 v 16-20; Philippians 4 v 10-13

# Journal

CHAPTER ELEVEN

# Coming to the End of Yourself

"We are ... struck down, but not destroyed"

2 CORINTHIANS 4 V 8-9

He is laying exhausted in a dank, dark cave, the sweat of suffering coating his brow, as he cries out for deliverance from the enemies who are pursuing him.

*How long, O LORD? Will you forget me forever?*
*How long will you hide your face from me?*
*How long must I take counsel in my soul*
*and have sorrow in my heart all the day?*
*How long shall my enemy be exalted over me? (Psalm 13 v 1-2)*

This is David, one of the greatest people in the history of God's people, the man who will one day rule Israel and conquer Jerusalem. But for now that all lies in the future. Here, he is pouring out his frustration and distress, unsure if he will see the light of another day. He is hiding himself from the ruthless Saul, the jealous king of Israel who wants to murder David so he cannot succeed to the throne. And the thought is crossing David's mind that maybe God has hidden his face and will not help.

Yet something beautiful is happening to David during this lonely and tortured scene in the cave. Rather than rejecting God and despairing of hope, he is drawn in his suffering to the throne of the only One who can save him. In Psalm 13, he teaches us how to do same.

## Where He Wants Us to Be

Like David, our brother Paul knew what it was to be overwhelmed by suffering. He was afflicted, perplexed, and persecuted... and he was "struck down."

Recall the last time suffering brought you to the end of yourself (perhaps it is doing so right now). Like David, you may have felt completely alone, rejected by God and abandoned in the darkness of your pain. Perhaps your desperate cries of "How long, O LORD?" only led to a deepening sorrow in your heart, as divine help seemed elusive, and deliverance from trouble a hopeless cause. Perhaps you gave up crying to God altogether.

Suffering brings us to the end of ourselves—our strength, our resources, our comfort, our understanding and wisdom, our plans and control—but as it does so, it can drive us to the One whose very being is endless. We often despise our limitations because we want to be strong and self-sufficient, but our weaknesses fit perfectly into God's gracious salvation plan. For it is only when we are bowed low before God in humility that we are exactly where he wants us to be and, surprisingly, where we most need to be—powerless to help ourselves and totally dependent upon him.

In Psalm 13, David has come to the end of himself and is literally at a dead end in the cave. Yet, what is true for him is true for us: the end of our self-sufficiency means the strengthening of God's gospel truths within us. We may be struck down, but we are not destroyed.

## Light and Love

The road to powerlessness is never easy because it goes against what we want and what our world values. But it has a beautiful destination.

David's suffering drew him to God, rather than driving him from God. But how? What did this look like? David drew near to God in the lowest point of his suffering for two reasons: he believed God's good plan to save him, and he trusted God's love.

*Draw near to God because he has saved you.* David's first plea is for God to protect him from his enemies—but there is more to this request than meets the eye. David prays, "Light up my eyes, lest I sleep the sleep of death" (Psalm 13 v 3). David wants to avoid death and defeat through the lighting up of his eyes. But how would light prevent his death? Shouldn't he ask God for a shield and a sword so he can defend himself, or for a way out of his enemy's path? Why does David pray, "Light up my eyes"?

Because he is praying for more than bodily protection (though he is not praying for less). He is pleading with God to sustain his faith in suffering.

> *Consider and answer me, O LORD my God;*
> *  light up my eyes, lest I sleep the sleep of death,*
> *lest my enemy say, "I have prevailed over him,"*
> *  lest my foes rejoice because I am shaken. (v 3-4)*

David knows that with intense suffering comes the temptation to reject God's abilities, purposes, and character. The most intense display of falling into that temptation is to walk away from the Lord. Unless God lights up his eyes to the hope of his salvation in the midst of his troubles, David will perish in this sleep of death. His faith will be destroyed, and the adversary of his soul will have won. So David prays for light.

In chapter 1, we saw that the light of Christ expels the darkness of sin and unbelief in a human heart, enabling someone who has been living in spiritual blindness to see the glory of Jesus (2 Corinthians 4 v 4-6). In the darkness of your suffering, when nothing else is clear to you and you feel completely struck down, God tells you to draw near to who and what you know to be true: the light of your salvation, Jesus Christ.

If you have trusted Christ to save your soul, even the most dire suffering will not lead you to ultimate destruction, but to the One who went through hell so you would never have to. Suffering will not lead you to hopelessness, but to the God of hope. It will not lead your faith to be shattered, but to an unshakeable hope that is founded on an immoveable Rock: Christ Jesus.

And we plant our feet firmly on that Rock and live in that Light when we are seeking Christ in his word. That's where we are reminded of and grow excited about his glory. When you are hurting, there's an understandable tendency to grow lazy in your pursuit of truth, to let the discipline of reading the Bible regularly slip because you are weary and feel jaded by your pain and feel burdened by the "Why?" questions. But there is no greater time to fight for faith! The more we soak in his word, and the more we believe the word we are soaking in, the more we will see Christ, and the stronger our faith will become. If it has been a while since you last opened your Bible, or a while since you felt that opening your Bible was anything more than a dry chore, open it now and as you read, pray, "O Lord my God, light up my eyes to the glory of Christ!"

*Draw near to God because he loves you.* The second reason that both David's and Paul's sufferings lead them nearer to God, rather than destroying them, is because they trust that his love is steadfast, even in pain. David sings:

> *But I have trusted in your steadfast love;*
>   *my heart shall rejoice in your salvation.*
> *I will sing to the LORD,*
>   *because he has dealt bountifully with me. (v 5-6)*

God's love changes the meaning of suffering for those in his care. We now see hardship through the eternal lens of his goodness toward us. David says, *I am thankful because you have saved my soul. By saving my soul, you have shown me the faithfulness of your love. And because I know that you are faithful, I trust that you will make good of everything else that comes my way.* By trusting in God's steadfast love, David is able to praise him in the darkness of the cave, just as Paul is able to praise God in the chains of imprisonment. Their questions and cries draw them to the God whose ultimate answer to being struck down, even in death, is "life!"

Fighting for this joy in times of darkness is a battle, but fight we must. The only other way is defeat and despair. One of the ways we can do this is by focusing on how God has "dealt bountifully" with us—what the great sixteenth-century Reformer Martin Luther (who knew more than his share of physical pain and psychological pressure) calls "the rhetoric of the Spirit." Luther was determined...

> *if a cross comes, to make the cross but little, but if there is a mercy, to make the mercy great.* (Cited in *The Rare Jewel of Christian Contentment* by Jeremiah Burroughs, page 155)

It is so easy to magnify our trials and to belittle our blessings. We can easily be defined by our pain and view everything else, including the mercy God gives us, through its dim prism; rather than defining ourselves by God's mercy, and seeing all else in that glorious light.

So pause now and think. What great and loving mercies has God brought to you? These will be different for all of us, but think about them. Has he given you food to eat? A family to love? Has he shown you compassion through fellow Christians? Has he revealed a fresh truth to you in Scripture? Has he spared you from many years of wandering without him?

And what about his grace? Hasn't he lavished it upon you, along with every spiritual blessing in the heavenly places? Hasn't he given you the Holy Spirit? Hasn't he promised never to leave you or forsake you? Hasn't he made you a co-heir with Christ? Hasn't he taken away your sin and forgiven your trespasses? Hasn't he spoken to you through his word? Hasn't he given you light to see the glory of Christ? Hasn't he set eternity with him before you?

Our crosses have come, and sometimes terribly so and without end in this life. But God has dealt bountifully with us. His mercies are greater, and his mercies are without end in eternity.

## Letting Suffering Draw Us Near

Friend, when you are in the darkness of the cave with David, and you begin to question God's love for you, remember what is true: Jesus Christ was sent into the world because God loves you. There is no greater demonstration of his affection for you, and there is no clearer proof that he intends to made good of what you are enduring right now. The One who was struck down on the cross is the One who could not be destroyed and, because he is for you, neither will you be.

He is your light. Draw near to him.

# Reflect

~ In what ways has God made you more obviously dependent on him through your trials? How has this dependence been good for your relationship with him?

~ How is your Bible-reading at the moment? Do you need to recommit to opening God's word regularly so you can soak in his truth and draw near to him there?

# Pray

*Lord Jesus, you are my light. Light up my eyes, lest I sleep the sleep of death in these trials. I want to draw near to you in my sufferings, and not wander from you. Protect me! Make my faith stronger as a result of these troubles, and reveal to me all the wonderful mercies that are mine because of your work on the cross. Give me a deeper grasp of how much you love me, and how you have proven this love in the gospel. Amen.*

*For further meditation:* 1 Samuel 1 v 1-20; Psalm 62 v 8; Psalm 118

**Journal**

_____
_____
_____
_____
_____
_____
_____
_____
_____
_____
_____
_____
_____
_____
_____
_____
_____
_____
_____
_____
_____
_____
_____
_____

CHAPTER TWELVE

# Beyond Bitter, Avoiding Numb

"We are ... struck down, but not destroyed"

2 CORINTHIANS 4 V 8-9

There is one common thread in the lives of those who endure a wilderness experience of pain and suffering: we will be changed by it, for better or for worse. Being struck down is hard. To the world it is a catastrophe. But while pain is never welcome, to the believer it's an opportunity to enter a landscape that often contains the most fertile ground for growth.

One way or another, suffering transforms us. We have a choice in how we'll respond to it. Such experiences will drive us in one of three directions: toward bitterness, or numbness, or a humble dependence upon Christ.

Over the last several years, I have been walking through a wilderness experience which has seemed unending. Enduring my eldest child's special needs along with the Lyme disease that all four children suffer from, while battling with my own health problems and financial strains has at its best challenged my family; at its worst it has nearly destroyed my family. I can clearly identify moments when I have responded in bitterness, and others where I have embraced numbness, as well as times when these trials have driven me into both a deeper understanding of the gospel and a greater love for Jesus. Our challenge is to recognize the moments of choice, and to choose by God's grace to grow toward him, not away from him.

## Better Than Bitterness

The path toward bitterness often begins with genuine pain and heartache coming from a deep sense of loss, hurt, or confusion. As painful and perplexing circumstances keep coming, and we feel as though we've been kicked when we are already down, bitterness knocks on our door masked as justifiable anger over the unfairness of life. When we are struck down by suffering we can't make sense of, we tend to frantically search for something or someone to blame. Since God is in control, he is an easy Someone to pin the blame on—to grow bitter towards as we stew inside, feeling as though we drew the short straw, or rather, that he gave us the short straw.

Psalm 73 portrays how easily we are led down this path toward bitterness:

*Behold, these are the wicked;*
*always at ease, they increase in riches.*
*All in vain I have kept my heart clean*
*and washed my hands of innocence.*
*For all the day long I have been stricken*
*and rebuked every morning ...*
*When my soul was embittered,*
*when I was pricked in heart,*
*I was brutish and ignorant;*
*I was like a beast toward you. (Psalm 73 v 12-14, 21-22)*

The troubling truth is that at the root of bitterness is unbelief and pride. Pride says, "I don't deserve this," or "I know what's best for me and I would be better off if I were in control of my circumstances." Unbelief says, "I don't believe God can be good if this is my lot."

I remember crying aloud in anger after watching my child cause emotional and physical destruction within our home, bringing me, my husband, and our other children to tears. I saw and felt the fear, anguish, and confusion rise up within each of us. This time, rather than falling to my knees in prayer and desperation, I angrily murmured, "This isn't fair! What did I do to deserve this?! I don't want to do this anymore—

I want out!" I could feel bitterness taking root within my heart. And the flower of bitterness toward God is rejection of God.

How do we combat bitterness when everything within us hates what is happening to us?

*But when I thought how to understand this,*
*  it seemed to me a wearisome task,*
*until I went into the sanctuary of God;*
*  then I discerned their end ...*
*Nevertheless, I am continually with you;*
*  you hold my right hand.*
*You guide me with your counsel,*
*  and afterward you will receive me to glory.*
*Whom have I in heaven but you?*
*  And there is nothing on earth that I desire besides you.*
*My flesh and my heart may fail,*
*  but God is the strength of my heart and my portion forever.*
*                                              (Psalm 73 v 16-17, 23-26)*

When we are bitter, we are saying to God, "You should have given me a better life than this. I want what I deserve!' and God says to us, often gently, sometimes firmly, *I have given you a better life than this, a better life than you can imagine, and I'm leading you to it. And I want for you what you don't deserve—eternal life.*

We can be, and must be, honest with the Lord about our feelings of bitterness, but then we must go to the truth of who he is and what he has done for us. We can combat an embittered heart by bringing it before the holy, compassionate, and all-satisfying presence of God. As we do that, he takes us by the hand, guides us into truth, and reminds us of the glorious eternity that awaits us. By his grace, despite our unbelief and pride, the Lord takes our misguided emotions and failing hearts and fills us with his strength and presence. The truth of the eternal hope we have in Christ washes our broken and bitter hearts with his undeserved forgiveness and faithfulness.

Friend, if you recognize bitterness growing within you, look to the cross of Jesus Christ. The circumstances that feel unfair, cruel, and pointless will begin to lose their power when we remember that our sinless Savior paid the penalty for our sin on the cross and bore all our griefs and sorrows. While bitterness says, "I don't deserve this," the gospel says, "You deserve far worse than this but have been forgiven, freed, and promised a glorious eternity with Christ." Bitterness is powerless and empty when transformed by the light of the gospel.

## A Way out of Numbness

Numbness presents itself as a more acceptable form of unbelief and rebellion than bitterness. Numbness temporarily blocks out and dulls the pain in order to avoid it at all costs.

For me, this temptation has come whenever the pain has felt like it's too much to bear. It manifests itself through things like watching too much television, eating more (and unhealthier) food, taking naps rather than getting things done, praying and reading the Bible less, avoiding conversation, not seeking the help I need, or looking for any immediate gratification that would cover the pain for even a moment. Numbness is about escaping or blocking out the hurt, rather than seeking to depend on Christ in that hurt.

No matter how we try to numb our pain, whether through temporary pleasures, seemingly innocent time wasters, or drugs and alcohol, the act can lead us into bondage and away from the blessings Christ desires to pour out on us through the very pain we are avoiding.

How do we combat numbness? We must first recognize it for what it is. If you are feeling knocked down in a season of suffering, evaluate how you spend your time. Do you find yourself drowning out the pain with something else? Excessive activity, unhealthy exercise or eating, more television, over-sleeping, computer time, reading unedifying books, compulsive shopping, hoarding, over-working, alcohol, drugs, or even pornography? At the same time, do you find yourself avoiding time in God's word and prayer?

> But for me it is good to be near to God;
> I have made the Lord GOD my refuge,

that I may tell of all your works. (Psalm 73 v 28)

Let us then with confidence draw near to the throne of grace, that we may receive mercy and find grace to help in time of need.
(Hebrews 4 v 16)

We don't have to pull ourselves together and package our feelings in a box with a pretty bow before coming to Christ. He can handle our raw emotions and wants us to bring them to him in honesty. We may fool ourselves and those around us, but Christ already knows the true state of our hearts and still wants us to draw near to him, confidently, even with all our messy, doubting, and faithless emotions.

So in times of brokenness, don't let the temptation to run away—to numb it all out—win. Come to Jesus in prayer, bring your emotions before him, and ask him for the grace you need to press on through the trials.

## Depend on Christ

So how do we keep from succumbing to bitterness and numbness when we are struck down by sin and the painful circumstances that enter our lives? We must take all our emotion, pain, confusion, and questions to Jesus Christ, our High Priest, who knows us intimately and can sympathize as One who has endured far more than we ever could imagine. What does this look like?

*Pray.* We cannot do any of this on our own. We need the strength of the Spirit to even see our tendency toward bitterness and numbness. We must begin with a simple prayer of dependency: "Hear, O Lord, when I cry aloud; be gracious to me and answer me!" (Psalm 27 v 7)

*Seek.* Make time in the Bible a priority every day. Surround yourself with believers who will encourage you and speak truth into your life. Fill your mind with wisdom from godly men and women who proclaim Christ's power, grace, and sufficiency in suffering. If we do not put guardrails of truth around ourselves in suffering, we will easily be swayed toward either bitterness or numbness. But with the truth of God's word, we will be strengthened, equipped, and transformed to reflect the image of Christ. "You have said, 'Seek my face.' My heart says to you, 'Your face, LORD, do I seek'" (Psalm 27 v 8).

*Wait.* Wait with anticipation. God does not waste a moment of our pain, and he will be faithful to provide what we need, give us strength to endure, and ultimately bring us forth as gold. You are a conqueror in Christ and must remind yourself of it constantly! We need not fear or despair, even when everything around us seems bleak and hopeless. We may be struck down, but we will not be destroyed. As David prayed:

> *I believe that I shall look upon the goodness of the LORD*
> *in the land of the living!*
> *Wait for the LORD;*
> *be strong, and let your heart take courage;*
> *wait for the LORD! (Psalm 27 v 13-14)*

## Reflect

~ Are you tempted more toward bitterness or numbness?
~ Is the Spirit convicting you of an area of sin that has become a way to avoid pain or run from what God is doing in your life?
~ Will you take steps today to pray, seek, and wait upon the Lord?

## Pray

*Jesus, I'm overwhelmed, hurting, confused, and want to escape this pain. Please forgive me and protect me from a heart of bitterness and numbness. Forgive me for not trusting your love and control over what you have allowed in my life. Help me not to run from these things, but to trust your love for me so I might persevere, endure, and find hope, peace, and joy in the midst of it. Don't waste this pain, but help me to know you more through it. Amen.*

*For further meditation:* 2 Corinthians 10 v 3-6

# Journal

CHAPTER THIRTEEN

# The Lonely Path to the Summit

"[We are] always carrying in the body the death of Jesus, so that the life of Jesus may also be manifested in our bodies. For we who live are always being given over to death for Jesus' sake, so that the life of Jesus also may be manifested in our mortal flesh"

2 CORINTHIANS 4 V 10-11

Many roads of suffering are incredibly lonely ones. Yes, it is true that there is nothing new under the sun (Ecclesiastes 1 v 9), and often there are more people who can relate to our suffering than we realize. Nevertheless, these roads are still isolated.

Paul summarizes all that he is facing in two phrases—he is "carrying in the body the death of Jesus," but not without purpose, for it is "so that the life of Jesus may also be manifested in our bodies." Following a suffering and rejected Savior in a fallen world will involve suffering—both because the world is fallen and because the world rejects its King. But when we suffer and choose to trust Christ through the trials we face, we are filled with his power and presence, reflecting his image to those around us.

The road of hurt is marked by hope. But we shouldn't underestimate that this road can, at times, be lonely. It was for Jesus, and it will be for those who follow in his steps.

I remember when we began realizing that my eldest son struggled in ways that other children seemed not to. When the struggles turned into life-altering challenges, I left social events, stores, and church feeling increasingly lonely. I was on a scary journey that it seemed no one else could relate to.

As the struggle intensified, I found myself pulling away from those I cared about, staying home, and pushing down the stress and emotional turmoil building within me. In the confusion, fear, and uncertain future, I felt utterly alone. Yes, there were those who tried to ask questions, offer their suggestions or share ways in which they could relate, but it always fell short of any real solace. No one could truly enter into the pain, heartache, and loneliness growing in my home and within my heart.

But—and I still find this surprising, and wonderful—over these lonely years I have discovered within me a thankfulness for the lonely road I have been given to travel. Walking it has brought me a greater understanding of what it means to be a follower of Jesus Christ and to know him not only as my Savior, but my comfort, sustainer, hope, and strength. There's something about having our worldly comforts stripped away, and company around us falling away, that allows us to begin to experience the true depth, length, and height of his love for us.

But this doesn't happen automatically; at least it didn't for me. My experience of walking the hard path, as well as knowing others close to me who walk it, has taught me that there are particular lies about loneliness that the devil whispers in our ear, and you and I need to learn to recognize and confront them with truth.

## Comfort in Christ

*The Lie:* Loneliness means I am alone.

*The Truth:* Loneliness strips away the external comfort found in those around me, driving me to find comfort in Christ alone.

> *Blessed be the God and Father of our Lord Jesus Christ, the Father of mercies and God of all comfort, who comforts us in our affliction...*
>
> *(2 Corinthians 1 v 3-4)*

We think about this verse more in chapter 15. Here, notice that yes, there are times when God allows us to feel alone, with the purpose of driving us deeper into his word and to prayer in search of a hope-filled and life-giving relationship with him. There is only one God of all comfort, and he does not sleep in your house or park next to you outside your church. He is Jesus. We cannot find true and lasting comfort in anyone but him, and when he is all we have left to turn to, we discover he should have been the first one we turned to.

By removing the earthly comfort of those around us, the Lord moves us in one of two directions: toward a deeper intimacy with our Savior, or toward the unveiling of an unrepentant heart—one which ultimately desires comfort more than Christ. So if you feel alone in your suffering, thank God that he loves you enough to allow this time in your life to draw you nearer to him.

## Christ Walked This Road

*The Lie:* I am the only one who has suffered like this, and no one will ever be able to understand my pain.

*The Truth:* Christ will not ask me to suffer anything he himself has not already suffered.

One reason why temptation arises is because we often don't know many people, if any, in our immediate circle of friends, family, or even acquaintances who have been called to endure the specific burden that we've been given to carry. Even if we meet someone whose trials are similar, different temperaments and previous experiences mean our reactions are still not the same. It becomes very easy to live resentfully, because no one understands. And yet there is One who is familiar with pain, who walked a harder path, who knows yours and mine, and who walks before and beside us.

> *He was despised and rejected by mankind, a man of suffering, and familiar with pain.*
> *As one from whom men hide their faces he was despised, and we esteemed him not. (Isaiah 53 v 3)*

Jesus Christ is the only one who can enter into our pain, fully and completely. He alone knows our hearts, temperaments, insecurities, fears, emotions, and desires. Jesus knows the pain of loneliness. He knows the loneliness of being misunderstood, the loneliness of being rejected by his own family, the loneliness of praying in agony while his closest friends drifted off to sleep nearby, and the loneliness of being abandoned by his Father. *And he did it all for you.* We may experience loneliness on many levels but because he went before us, we will never have to experience the crushing loneliness of separation from God the Father, as he did. Our loving Father sent his own Son down the loneliest road ever known to man so that we would never have to walk any road apart from him.

When you are tempted to withdraw, realize that Christ alone can fill the deep holes left by the heartaches of life. He knows, he understands, he cares and he can comfort. By his Spirit, he is with us. Our Savior does not comfort us by cheering us on from a distance. Instead, he lives within us and walks beside us, even as he beckons us on down the Calvary road.

## The Summit is Glorious

*The Lie:* I will always feel alone.

*The Truth:* The loneliness of this life will quickly fade as we unite and rejoice for eternity with our brothers and sisters in Christ, giving glory to God for who he is and all he has done.

Follow after Jesus, and one day you will no longer have to walk this lonely road. You will be with your Savior, face to face, in perfect fellowship and unity with every other believer—past, present, and future. Imagine experiencing this, as best you can; one day it will be reality, not longing:

> *Then I heard what seemed to be the voice of a great multitude, like the roar of many waters and like the sound of mighty peals of thunder, crying out, "Hallelujah! For the Lord our God the Almighty reigns. Let us rejoice and exult and give him the glory, for the marriage of the Lamb has come, and his Bride has made herself ready; it was granted her to clothe herself with fine linen, bright and pure"—for the fine linen is*

*the righteous deeds of the saints. And the angel said to me, "Write this: Blessed are those who are invited to the marriage supper of the Lamb."*
*(Revelation 19 v 6-9)*

This gives me such hope. Although this road of following Christ can feel so lonely at times, we know it won't be forever. When Christ calls his people home, we will be gathered with a great multitude of saints and we will praise his name together. Unity, empathy, acceptance and joy will replace the isolation and loneliness. Christ will have crushed the enemy and all his evil schemes to drown us in hopelessness and despair, freeing us once and for all from the loneliness of suffering, and from being misunderstood, mocked, persecuted, excluded, or rejected by those we love.

There are some incredibly painful, long, lonely roads that some of us are asked to walk. Perhaps you are walking down one today. Although you may feel alone, and sometimes are alone in terms of those around you, Christ has walked the lonely road to Calvary so that you would never have to walk any road apart from him. One day, the road will end, and it will end in the eternal city of God's people. The loneliness of this world will be washed away in the presence of Christ. The path is uphill, but the summit is glorious.

## Reflect

~ Have you found yourself believing any of these lies in your own season of loneliness?

~ Will you take the time to address lies you have believed and speak truth into them?

~ Will you allow the loneliness you feel to drive you deeper into the loving and strong arms of Christ?

~ Is Christ worth following, even if it means a life of loneliness?

# Pray

*"Who is the man who fears the LORD? Him will he instruct in the way that he should choose. His soul shall abide in well-being, and his offspring shall inherit the land. The friendship of the LORD is for those who fear him, and he makes known to them his covenant. My eyes are ever toward the LORD, for he will pluck my feet out of the net. Turn to me and be gracious to me, for I am lonely and afflicted. The troubles of my heart are enlarged; bring me out of my distresses. Consider my affliction and my trouble, and forgive all my sins." Amen. (Psalm 25 v 12-18)*

*For further meditation:* Matthew 11 v 25-30; 27 v 46; Luke 14 v 25-33; 17 v 5-6

*Journal*

CHAPTER FOURTEEN

*Never Without Purpose*

"So death is at work in us, but life in you"

2 CORINTHIANS 4 V 12

When pain is particularly tragic or terrifying, when it is permanent rather than momentary, there's a thought that we don't often talk about, but we need to: *Why am I still alive? Why can't God just let me die?*

Why does God not take the suffering out of us, or us out of our suffering? Why does he leave his people in the midst of pain?

When Paul writes about the "death" that is "at work" in him and his Christian friends, he is speaking of the daily act of self-denial by which he joyfully and willingly follows the crucified Christ, even through suffering and sacrifice, and even to the point of death. At this time in Paul's life, God has willed that he remain alive and fruitful for the gospel, despite imprisonment and other perpetual, brutal sufferings that resulted from his faithful preaching. Certainly, God is teaching him how to live for and depend on Christ in the midst of his daily deaths-to-self. But the "life" Paul is talking about in this verse is actually not about the life that is "in him," but "in you."

It is about the church.

In a different letter, to the church in Philippi, he writes:

*It is my eager expectation and hope that I will not be at all ashamed, but that with full courage now as always Christ will be honored in my body, whether by life or by death. For to me to live is Christ, and to die is gain. If I am to live in the flesh, that means fruitful labor for me. Yet which I shall choose I cannot tell. I am hard pressed between the two. My desire is to depart and be with Christ, for that is far better. But to remain in the flesh is more necessary on your account. Convinced of this, I know that I will remain and continue with you all, for your progress and joy in the faith, so that in me you may have ample cause to glory in Christ Jesus, because of my coming to you again.*

*(Philippians 1 v 20-26)*

How does any of this help with the searing question of the sufferer: "Why can't God just let me die?" Think about the Christian who is instantly paralyzed by an accident, and then is bedridden for the rest of her days. Or the victim of a degenerative disease who slowly but surely loses her quality of life. What about the believer who feels trapped in an abusive relationship, or a home life that brings trouble upon trouble? What about the person who has lost a loved one to tragedy and cannot fathom how to live without him?

If Paul desires to depart and be with Christ, then why does God leave him in the body, with all his sufferings and hardships?

Because it is necessary for those around him. "My desire is to depart and be with Christ, for that is far better. But to remain in the flesh is more necessary on your account." *Oh, if I had my choice,* Paul says, *I would be in heaven with my Lord!* To be with Jesus is better than remaining in the body, for Paul and for us. When that happens what a day that will be! And what a wonderful way to look at death. To be with Christ is better by far. Yet God's word says that if we remain, it is because our work for him isn't finished.

Suffering Christian, you are alive today because God has a purpose for your pain that is for the good of others and the glory of Christ. Death-to-self may be at work in your suffering, but life-in-Christ is at work in the church.

## For the Good of Others

Paul's work for the church was obvious, as he was on the ground doing ministry. God was producing visible, abundant fruit through his perseverance. Perhaps some of us can relate to Paul, but many of us will not see as clearly how our perseverance in the body is bearing fruit. But if God is allowing us to live, we can be sure that he is also using our labor—even when we cannot understand the details or see the outcome. Every humble act of service is precious in God's sight.

God gives us material for sacrifice. Sometimes the sacrifice makes little sense to others, but when offered to him it is always accepted. The transformation into something he can use for the good of others takes place only when the offering is put into his hands.

Think about your circles of influence, especially those within the church. As you endure suffering with hope and remain in the body with perseverance, you are engaging in a necessary ministry; you have the opportunity to do good to the church by exalting Christ in your body, through your suffering and your service. In Paul's words, "I will remain and continue with you all, for your progress and joy in the faith."

You do good to the church by exalting Christ through your suffering. The person who holds fast to Christ in suffering has a magnetic faith. The church needs to know how to be content and joyful in hardship, and a believer who remains steadfast in trials is a living, breathing example of what this looks like. Faithful suffering spurs others on to praise God and bear the cost of living for him.

It is good for other believers to watch a suffering brother or sister treasure the things of heaven over the things of earth, and to live out the line from the psalm: "My flesh and my heart may fail, but God is the strength of my heart and my portion forever" (Psalm 73 v 26). It is good for Christians to be reminded that death has no victory or sting because our Lord defeated it at the cross. It is good for your church to witness a real-life parable of the truth that suffering need not—cannot—crush Christian joy.

As you struggle on, clinging to Christ even as you feel the foretaste of death each day, you are serving your church. They, and their Lord, will thank you for it in glory.

## Still Serving Others

You do good to the church by exalting Christ through your service. Christian, you are not defined by your suffering, but by your Savior. You are in Christ. God can certainly use your hurts, but your purpose goes far beyond them. He has prepared good works for you to do (Ephesians 2 v 10).

Perhaps that good work is to cling on to your faith under the most severe suffering. But if you are able to leave your bed, that good work will in some way mean serving your church, or working in your job faithfully, or parenting your children with steadfastness, or showing hospitality to neighbors, or laboring in prayer for others. It may be less than you would like, and less than you used to be able to give (imagine the frustration for Paul when. rather than preaching and planting churches, he was under guard in a prison). But you can still serve, and in God's good plans that service is necessary.

This is why Paul knew that it would be better to be with Christ; yet it was more necessary to live for Christ—even if he was in prison.

The same is true for accepting the service of others. Christ is exalted when we humble ourselves to receive the good works and prayerful labor of other Christians. Our suffering is an opportunity for others to grow in Christ-like humility by helping us. We need to be open and willing and humble to allow them that privilege.

If you woke up with breath in your lungs today, it is because God's purpose for you on this earth is not finished. It is necessary that you remain in the physical body, for the good of the spiritual body of our Lord Jesus.

## Bringing Glory to Christ

From the ailing believer who relies on God's provision to take one more breath, to the hard-pressed single mother who continues to serve her family faithfully, our daily deaths in the body point to the everlasting resurrection life that Jesus gives us, and to the beautiful, freeing truth that, in every circumstance, he is enough for us. "So death is at work in us, but life in you."

Because our suffering makes our service a greater challenge, anything we do is more obviously seen as Christ working in and through us. And because our suffering robs us of certain good, earthly gifts, we showcase more clearly what is of ultimate value in the next life—that Jesus Christ is our gain. As we carry his death in our bodies, and his power works through us, his all-surpassing value shines forth.

Suffering is a chance to exalt Christ—so a life that includes suffering is one well worth living. Suffering is a chance to serve your church—you likely have no idea how you are provoking, challenging and comforting those around you. Death may be at work in you through pain and hardship, but life is at work in others as you exalt Christ in your body. In leaving you in suffering, God is choosing for you a necessary ministry, and an impactful life, before he takes you home to be with him.

If you woke up with breath in your lungs today, it is because God's purpose for you on this earth is not finished. It is necessary that you remain in the physical body, for the glory of Jesus Christ and the good of his church.

## Reflect

~ Think about your areas of influence. Whose lives do you touch? Ask the Lord how he would continue to use you and give yourself wholly to his service, whatever it looks like.

~ When we are hurting, our opportunities to serve and influence others can be hard to see. Ask someone close to you about where they think God has gifted and placed you for service.

~ If you are ready to depart and be with Jesus today, would you ask him to be glorified through your life right now? Would you trust him for his timing and plans?

# Pray

*All-sufficient God, there are days when I just want to be home in heaven with you. You know this. It is not hidden from your sight. But I don't want to miss how you might use me here. So I'm asking for clarity about how I might serve others amid this pain. Through your Spirit, help me love others, consider others, and walk before others with hope in Christ. Use me for your glory until you call me home. Amen.*

*For further meditation:* Isaiah 55 v 6-9; Psalm 46

# Journal

CHAPTER FIFTEEN

*How to Offer Real Comfort*

"Since we have the same spirit of faith according to what
has been written, 'I believed, and so I spoke,' we also
believe, and so we also speak, knowing that he who raised
the Lord Jesus will raise us also with Jesus and bring us
with you into his presence. For it is all for your sake, so
that as grace extends to more and more people it may
increase thanksgiving, to the glory of God"

2 CORINTHIANS 4 V 13-15

What brings you real comfort in a place of deep suffering and trial? Does someone telling you, "It will be all right," "I believe God will bring healing," "You're a strong person, I know you will get through this," or "I'll pray you get better and that this will all come to an end" bring you real, lasting comfort?

These statements always fall short of offering any real comfort. Though they sometimes carry partial truths—since it's good and right to pray for healing and better circumstances—they can also reinforce the misleading idea that our greatest problem is our suffering, and the removal of it would be God's greatest blessing.

In his book *The Call to Joy and Pain*, author Ajith Fernando says:

*I think one of the most serious blind spots in the western church is a defective understanding of suffering. We have a lot of teaching about escape from and therapy for suffering, but there is inadequate teaching about the theology of suffering.*

*One result of not having a proper theology of suffering is that we suffer more than we need to when we encounter pain or frustration. Living as we do in this fallen world, we can be certain that we will encounter suffering. It is so closely embedded into life on earth that no human can avoid it. If believers do not accept suffering as something out of which good will come, when they suffer they think something is seriously wrong. Comments from others can reinforce that idea. They get disillusioned with God and the church, or they struggle with unnecessary discouragement and doubt. You cannot have joy with such attitudes. (pages 51-52)*

In other words, if we do not have a correct theology of suffering, we will be shocked, devastated, and angered when adversity strikes us or those we love. What we really believe shapes what we actually say, both to ourselves and to others. If we believe the wrong thing, we will say the wrong thing, and end up resorting to quasi-Christian clichés (which offer false hope) or to never having anything to say at all to those who are hurting (which offers no hope).

Paul teaches us that no matter what circumstances or company we may find ourselves in, our message of hope should confidently remain the same. Trace his logic in these verses. He believes that Christ has risen to eternal life, and so one day he will raise Paul to eternal life. So this is what he speaks of, for the sake of his listeners coming to understand and appreciate grace, and the sake of his God coming to receive the thanksgiving he so richly and infinitely deserves.

If we believe in resurrection hope, we will speak that hope into the lives of others. One of the most crucial times for us to share this truth is when we are walking alongside a brother or sister who is suffering and struggling to see this hope for themselves. And what better person is there to share such hope than one who has been comforted and strengthened by it through their own season of suffering?

*Blessed be the God and Father of our Lord Jesus Christ, the Father of mercies and God of all comfort, who comforts us in all our affliction, so that we may be able to comfort those who are in any affliction, with the comfort with which we ourselves are comforted by God. For as we share abundantly in Christ's sufferings, so through Christ we share abundantly in comfort too. (2 Corinthians 1 v 3-5)*

Have you ever realized that if and as your afflictions lead you to cling to Christ, you are becoming someone who is qualified to speak to others of the comfort that you have received and that they can be strengthened and encouraged by?

## Christ's Comfort is Better Than Commiseration

As I have endured years of physical pain, heartache, and loss, I have come to learn that nothing can replace what's been lost, or repair what's been broken, apart from Christ. But instead of the Lord comforting me by removing the pain and reversing the loss of my worldly hopes, he has comforted me with his presence and secure future hope. In his grace, he has not only comforted me through his word and promises but through brothers and sisters in Christ who walk this journey with me. It is out of these comforts that I can turn to someone else and offer that same comfort.

Comforting another person in their pain is not simply commiserating with them, and it may not always mean agreeing with them. It is speaking the truths of the gospel that we ourselves have found of greater value than any earthly comfort. We need to point to God's promises while being real about the present. Instead of telling them it will be alright and life will get easier (you don't know that), we can comfort them with the truth that not a second of their pain will be wasted, and that when Christ returns, there will not be one more second of pain or heartache (you can know that!).

Although we may not be able to make sense of what someone else is going through, Christ promises that as they choose to trust him (even if their faith is hanging by a thread), he will faithfully use those trials to accomplish his good and loving purposes in their life and the lives of those around them. We may not be able to offer answers or temporary solutions that ease their pain, but we can bring the comfort of Christ and the eternal value of suffering with him.

## Christ's Comfort is Better Than Your Experience

Not everyone grieves or responds to suffering in the same way or time frame that we do. In fact, no one responds in exactly the same way as you do. So if we seek to comfort only through our own experiences, we are bound to say the wrong thing, offer nothing more than temporal comfort, and possibly even obscure or undo the gospel comfort others are seeking to share with them.

This is why, I think, we are often speechless and feel we have nothing to say when someone we love is hurting. But we do have something to say! Not out of our own reserves of wisdom or experience alone, but out of the treasures of the gospel.

So how does this look practically?

- ~ We need to be slow to judge whether they are suffering "well," and quick to grieve and mourn alongside of them.
- ~ We need to be slow to speak the "truths" we think they need to hear, and quick to discern and pray about encouraging them with Scripture and God's promises.
- ~ We need to be slow to impatience, and quick to learn how to be long-suffering.
- ~ We need to be slow to run away from the discomfort of entering another's pain, and quick to allow God to use their suffering to grow our own faith.
- ~ We need to be slow to speak our opinions and solutions, and quick to listen and hear their heart.
- ~ We need to be slow to do the minimum and quick to serve in ways God calls us to, even if it takes sacrifice. (This does not mean we must say yes to all needs!)
- ~ We need to be slow to view the other's suffering as their problem, and quick to see the other's suffering as a privilege in which we can love, serve, and be mutually blessed by the body of Christ.

~ We need to be slow to believe that we are aren't equipped to help and quick to comfort with the unique gifts and personality that God has given us. (If you are good at crafts, make an encouraging gift. If you are hands-on, offer to help with work around the house. If you like writing, send a note of how you see Christ working in their life.)

## You Are Not the Savior

You cannot fix it. Loving the hurting opens us up to the temptation to see ourselves as the sufferer's personal savior. But they do not need you—they need Christ. Comfort is about redirecting someone to seek what they need in Christ first and not in you. Comfort is not about always being there for someone; it is about reminding someone that Christ is always there for them. This frees us from a burden we weren't meant to carry. It frees us to speak truth and show love but not to feel guilty about what we cannot manage or cannot solve. You are not their Savior. God is not expecting you to be—he already sent Another to do that job.

So let's not be afraid to enter into someone else's pain and seek to speak gospel comfort to them. God's purpose in your trials may well be to qualify you to help another to cling to their Savior in their trials.

## Ready to Be Comforted?

Of course, this is all a two-way street. It is from the overflow of the comfort we find in knowing that Jesus has risen and will raise us too that we are able to comfort others. So be sure, in your suffering, to allow that comfort to sink deep into your heart. Speak of what you believe to yourself. And let others speak it to you, too. While they may not say it at just the moment when you want to hear it, or in just the way you would like to hear it, they say it because they believe it and because they love you.

# Reflect

~ In what ways have you been ministered to and comforted by another person?

~ If you are enduring a trial, do you have someone who can walk alongside you, not only with compassion but with wisdom to speak the truth of the gospel into your life? If not, will you seek someone?

~ Who has God placed in your path with whom you can share the comfort of Christ that you also have received, or are receiving, in your own season of suffering?

# Pray

*Father, I thank you that you are a God of compassion and comfort who comforts us in all our affliction. Thank you that you don't waste a moment of our suffering, but use it not only for your glory in our lives but in the lives of those around us. Help us to receive the comfort of others in the body of Christ as a provision and gift from you, and in turn to show that same comfort to those you put in our path. As your grace extends to more and more people, may it increase thanksgiving, to the glory of your name. Amen.*

*For further meditation:* Psalm 23 v 4-6; Psalm 71 v 20-21; Psalm 119 v 49-52; Matthew 5 v 4

# Journal

CHAPTER SIXTEEN

# How Suffering Can Change You for the Better

"So we do not lose heart. Though our outer self is wasting
away, our inner self is being renewed day by day"

2 CORINTHIANS 4 V 16

The marathon runner perseveres in her training in order to someday finish a grueling 26.2 mile race. The hesitant child presses on through eating her vegetables because she knows there is chocolate ice cream sitting in the freezer.

Perseverance is rooted in hope. We persevere when we believe that what awaits us is worth the fight.

After traversing the realities of earthly trouble in his letter to the Corinthians, showing how the hope of the gospel transforms a Christian's hurts, Paul's conclusion is simply this: "We do not lose heart." Jesus has risen and will bring us into his presence! Our hope in Christ is secure and unshakeable. The One who awaits us in glory is well worth the fight to get there.

But Paul's eyes are not only on the future. He knows that this fight of faith is accomplishing something else of great worth along the way: the renewing of our inner self, even while our outer self is wasting away. His point is this: that suffering changes us, for the better, right now.

That is hard to believe! Let's look together at Romans 5 v 1-5, where Paul helps us understand how this inner transformation happens and where it begins:

*Therefore, since we have been justified by faith, we have peace with God through our Lord Jesus Christ. Through him we have also obtained access by faith into this grace in which we stand, and we rejoice in hope of the glory of God. Not only that, but we rejoice in our sufferings, knowing that suffering produces endurance, and endurance produces character, and character produces hope, and hope does not put us to shame, because God's love has been poured into our hearts through the Holy Spirit who has been given to us. (Romans 5 v 1-5)*

## Renewal Begins with the Gospel

Renewal into the image of Christ begins with the gospel and then follows a progression from endurance to character to hope. Before we see how our inner self is renewed through this progression though, the passage leads us to look at where such renewal begins. We must know where we are headed, and why we are headed there, before we can understand the stops along the way.

Perseverance in the fight of faith does not happen on its own accord or by our efforts; rather, the gospel fuels it. Paul reminds us above that we have been justified by faith in Christ—given a verdict of "not guilty" and declared completely innocent by the Judge of all things on the basis of Christ's perfect life and sin-bearing death. This means that we now have "peace with God through our Lord Jesus Christ" and access into his grace—his undeserved favor—forever. Righteousness by faith, peace with God, and access into his grace form this greater gospel-reality that overflows into rejoicing because of our future in God's glorious presence. To be with Christ is guaranteed, and to be like him is our aim! "We rejoice in hope of the glory of God."

But these are not only wonderful treasures stored up for our future. They are for now. Right now, if you are trusting in Christ, you are justified before God. You are at peace with the only One whose verdict truly matters. You have access, through prayer, to the throne room of the universe whenever you wish to enter it.

And this enables you to stand in suffering. More than that, it means that you can be changed by suffering, for the better. As we persevere to the finish, this gospel produces renewal in us as we go.

## Suffering Produces Endurance

If the gospel is the fuel for inner change, then suffering is the uphill road we travel on. Suffering will cause us to do either one of two things: to give up on our faith, or to get in the fight of faith. To despair, or to persevere. To break down, or to press on. Suffering exercises our faith muscles, and exercise makes muscles grow stronger even as sometimes they feel weaker.

Think about our marathoner. Her body will suffer many weeks of training, and must suffer many weeks of training, if she is to endure to the end of the race. Her muscles will stretch and ache, so that they may be rebuilt, grow stronger, and sustain her to the finish line. Then she will have become an endurance runner.

Similarly, in suffering our faith muscles are tested and tried, in order that God may strengthen and sustain our faith until the day we are with him and faith turns to sight. The longer I suffer, and the more I am able to persevere in that suffering (with rejoicing!), the more deeply I am convinced that Jesus Christ is the author and perfecter of faith. When the road is steep and my faith feels weak but I keep going, my faith is growing stronger. I am becoming an endurance believer.

It is hard to believe by faith what God has promised us in Christ Jesus when all we can see is hardship and pain. It is hard to trust that God's character is indeed good and faithful when our circumstances seem anything but. It is hard to see our obstacles as gifts of grace that grow us when they feel like obstacles to faith that discourage us. Suffering produces a stronger faith in God's promises because everything else we lean on—everything that makes up the "outer self"—is being exposed and stripped away.

Our suffering also produces endurance as we obey God's commands. Because of self-pity, discontentment, anger, bitterness, and other sinful fruit, suffering often tempts us to turn away from God's commands by indulging our present feelings as we demand our "rights" to a better life. Yet, when we turn away from sin and pursue obedience to God, our faith is strengthened, and we recognize how he is working within us.

We cannot do these two things in our own strength. Nor do we have to! This is why the Holy Spirit has been given to us, Paul says. He works in us what we cannot work in ourselves. The Holy Spirit first made us alive to God's love, and he will also strengthen our endurance in the fight of faith to the end.

## Endurance Produces Character

Suffering changes the sufferer. No doubt you've met people who have been made hard, angry, timid or bitter by suffering. Wonderfully, the Spirit is at work to change our character for the better. Holiness increases as we endure suffering by the Spirit. We will get into some specific examples of what this holiness looks like in the next few chapters. For now, we see that endurance produces character as the Holy Spirit pours God's love into our hearts; and the fruit of the Spirit is love, joy, peace, patience, kindness, goodness, faithfulness, gentleness, and self-control (Galatians 5 v 22-23).

As the Holy Spirit grows our inner self through endurance, more of our outer self is put to death. We learn what it is to truly *love* God, rather than loving only what he gives us. We learn to know *joy* in suffering, rather than looking for happiness in temporary pleasures. We learn *patience* as we suffer long and wait for the Lord's return; *kindness* toward others that humbly serves them through the pain; *goodness* as we learn to hate sin and all its effects; *faithfulness* as we focus on God's promises to lead us through; *gentleness* as our affliction teaches us to comfort and identify with fellow sufferers; and *self-control* as we learn to meekly submit ourselves to God's loving plans for us, despite our lack of understanding of what he is doing and why.

The world and all its glamours are fading away. This includes our bodies, money, possessions, aspirations, and positions. We cannot keep what we now see, but we will possess forever what we cannot see.

## Character Produces Hope

There comes a moment for most marathon runners when they realize they will make it, because they realize their training has done what they planned—turned them into real endurance runners. Well, what rejoicing there is when we realize that our faith is indeed genuine and gospel-fueled, and that the Holy Spirit is producing Christ-like character in us! When the road goes uphill, when our faith feels weak but proves strong enough, when we see the Spirit changing us bit by bit along the way, we realize: We are justified! We do have peace with God. We can and we will enjoy access to his grace! Our hope is real. This is how you rejoice even during—and perhaps especially during—times of suffering.

"Though our outer self is wasting away, our inner self is being renewed day by day." Suffering changes our outer self—it scars, it pains, it reshapes, it breaks. Look at the outer self and you will lose heart. But Paul doesn't—because he looks elsewhere. The road of suffering changes our inner self too, as we cling to the gospel and the Spirit goes to work. That's where you must look.

## Reflect

~ What aspects of your outer self do you tend to focus on? How does suffering tend to shift your focus?

~ What changes in your inner self have you discerned through times of suffering?

~ How does the gospel fuel your hope as you travel the road of suffering?

# Pray

*Father God, your word says you are using my suffering to renew me, but I often get so discouraged in the hurt that I don't easily see this. Open my eyes to know how you have already changed my heart, and how you still want to change me. Please produce in me an enduring faith that proves to be genuine through these trials. Grow good fruit in me, and get rid of the bad fruit that I know is often there. Help me to love you and to love what you are producing more than I love comfort and answers. In Jesus' name, Amen.*

*For further meditation:* Job 23 v 8-12; Hebrews 12 v 3-11; 1 Peter 4 v 19

## Journal

## CHAPTER SEVENTEEN

# The Freedom of Not Being in Control

"So we do not lose heart. Though our outer self is wasting away, our inner self is being renewed day by day"

2 CORINTHIANS 4 V 16

*S*ubmission is not a popular word. For many of us, there's an instinctive cringe or resistance at the mention of it. Why is that? Very simply put, we like control. We like knowing what to expect and we like carefully planning our course so that we achieve our desired outcome. When we lose our sense of control, we tend to become frazzled or afraid. We like to be in charge, and not to submit to anything or anyone else.

Except that sometimes, we love it! There are times that it's wonderful not to be in control. Maybe there's been a time when you were exhausted and overwhelmed with the kids, and your mom or friend came over and took charge, possibly even forcing you to sit down and rest! Or maybe you were overwhelmed with a project at work that was above your capabilities, and your boss took the lead to guide you successfully through it. In these moments, there comes a point when you realize that you are beyond your limits and you need help, and you're thankful rather than annoyed or fearful that someone else takes control.

Christians are those who accept Jesus as Lord. But when it comes to submitting to him as Lord, especially when we are faced with unfavorable circumstances and the wasting away of our outer selves, it's hard to let go of the control we desire. I don't really want my outer self to waste away. And when it does, I lose heart.

For me, the choice of whether to submit or resist, to surrender control or to seek to seize control, is a daily, moment-by-moment one. I have battled for much of my life with pain and sickness in one form or another. In fact, not long ago, I began seeing yet another doctor after being incredibly discouraged from years of struggling with my health, with no answers found. As I battle through each day, I often feel weary and discouraged, struggling to accept why God has chosen to give me this constant physical strife with everything else that is on my plate. Many days I grieve inwardly (and often outwardly), keenly aware of the hopes and desires I have but lack the energy to accomplish. I am often tempted to live in the miserable mind trap of pain.

## Will I Trust the Doctor?

Through my own recent struggles, I have been given an illustration of how submission looks and why it is good. The Lord has brought me to a new level of dependency upon him over the last few weeks as my new doctor has given me a strict diet of porridge, and porridge only, for the next two or three months in an attempt to heal my stomach. Have you ever eaten the same bland thing for more than a day? It's a constant battle as I cook for my family, unable to eat that food myself, and feel left out of the many activities that often surround food.

Every day, I have to choose whether to lay down my will and desire to eat what I want, and submit to the will of the doctor for the hope of long-term health; or else indulge in the short-term pleasure of cheating, at the cost of possible freedom from this illness.

God doesn't waste anything in our lives. He is using this struggle in my own life to reveal in me how much I want control. After all, my doctor is not aimlessly asking me to submit my desires for food to her eating plan just because she can, or for some kind of bad joke. She is asking me to trade in my current comfort and enjoyment in food for the hope of something greater—the hope of healing. So I have to ask myself, *Can I, will I, trust the doctor?*

And this is a small picture of the way the Lord works in our lives. He is the Creator and Sustainer of our lives, and he alone knows what will ultimately bring about the transformation of our heart, mind, and soul—our inner selves. Often, this process involves giving up control, giving up our sense that we can affect the outcome of our lives, giving up what's desirable and easy, giving up what we are used to enjoying.

## Do Not Lose Heart

At these points, the question is: *Can I, will I, trust God?*

*Yes.* Because of who God is, there is sweet freedom in laying everything down. Our hopes, dreams, plans, health, past, present, and future. Not in defeated surrender, but in willing and humble submission, trusting his loving control and purpose over every aspect of our lives. After all, he has already proved that he holds nothing back in order to do what is best for us:

> *He who did not spare his own Son but gave him up for us all, how will he not also with him graciously give us all things? (Romans 8 v 32)*

If God was willing to not spare his own Son in order to save you, then he will not withhold anything that he knows you need for your eternal good. We serve a God who is for us, who will provide all we need, and who will somehow bring good from the evil and suffering that we experience on this earth as we submit to him, just as he did through Jesus' life, death, and resurrection.

> *Humble yourselves, therefore, under the mighty hand of God so that at the proper time he may exalt you. (1 Peter 5 v 6)*

At first glance, this verse can appear oppressive. But in fact it's freeing, because of whose hand we are under. As the pastor Juan Sanchez writes:

> *There is no safer place in the universe to be than under his mighty hand ... we are not entrusting ourselves to some unknowable, impersonal deity, but to our heavenly Father, who loves us and cares for us.*
>
> *(1 Peter For You, page 173)*

To humble ourselves under God's hand—to submit to his control—is simply to live in line with reality. The irony is that we never have had and never will have control, however much we may think we do or however hard we may work to have it. We are dependent beings. Every breath we take is a gift from our Creator.

So while submission sounds oppressive and being in control sounds freeing, in fact as creatures with a Creator, the opposite is true. When we fight to hold the reins, we get caught in an exhausting, stress-filled, joy-sucking cycle of trying to control what we don't have the power or wisdom to control. There is no freedom in that, but only a false confidence, leaving us prone to being tossed by the inevitable storms of life that will come our way. If suffering does nothing else, it reminds us that we are not in charge.

Complete trust in God's control, on the other hand, frees us—to serve, to rest, and to work in the way God has intended for us. Some days, that simply means choosing to serve, love, and trust our Savior in the quietness of our hearts amid seasons of pain and heartache.

I have no doubt that if I were able to hear each of your hearts, I would hear many different cries of suffering. Some of you have experienced the wasting away of your outer self through the loss of a loved one who was very much a part of you. Some of you have had a dream stripped away due to an injury, illness, or detour of life. Some of you are daily dealing with pain, cancer, or autoimmune diseases. Some of you are struggling with the places where your mind takes you. Some of you are battling many other challenges. None of them are easy. None of them were chosen. And yet none of them are out of control, for God is in control.

I would like to encourage you with the beautiful writings of Amy Carmichael, an incredibly godly and inspiring missionary woman born in the late 1800's. After years of serving the Lord in many different mission fields, she learned later to serve the Lord in the way of submission to him in a bed-ridden and painful state in the second half of her life. She wrote this letter to a young woman, who at the time was extremely ill, and was helpless to help those whom she loved. May you take heart in these words, as I have:

*Be at rest about the work. It is God's, not ours. May he not do as he will with his own work—supply it with what it seems to us to need so much, or denude it of just that? Yes, he may. (Is it not lawful for me to do what I will with mine own?)*

*Lord, thou mayest do as thou wilt with thine own. We trust thee, we love thee; the work is thine; not ours at all. We can only give to thee what thou givest us of strength, of wisdom, of ability for it. If thou takest these powers from us and makest us weak, so that we cannot help the work, if our children must be left without what we long to give them, Lord, it is thy matter, not ours. My child, it has meant much to me to come to this. Let not your heart be troubled, neither let it be afraid.*

## Reflect

~ In what ways has God allowed you to experience the wasting away of your outer self? In what ways have you seen him using that to renew your inner self?

~ If you are feeling as though life is going well and your plans are falling into place, would you bring everything to Christ in submission, asking him to show you what he desires for you today with your time, money, energy, and opportunities?

~ Are you discouraged? Have you felt unproductive and worthless due to illness, injury, or grief? Would you trust today that Christ is near and able to use even our greatest weaknesses for his glory if we offer all of ourselves in submission to his will? He will be faithful.

# Pray

Let's pray the closing words of Amy Carmichael's letter:

> "My God, I offer Thee all my thoughts, words, actions, and sufferings this day, for all the intentions of Thy divine heart." Amen.

*For further meditation:* Psalm 143 v 10; Matthew 26 v 42; John 5 v 30

## Journal

## CHAPTER EIGHTEEN

# God Is the Great Gardener

"So we do not lose heart. Though our outer self is wasting away, our inner self is being renewed day by day"

2 CORINTHIANS 4 V 16

'll never forget the week we lost our home. It was the home that we'd fallen in love with four years before, and we'd said we would never move again. And yet there we were, having to walk away from it all. Circumstances that we never saw coming had forced us to decide what we valued most in life, and to make some hard choices. For years we worked, sacrificed, and saved to have a home like that. Now someone else lives in it.

But God has a way of using painful circumstances such as these to move us in a direction we never would have chosen; such was the case for our family. While we felt the loss, we experienced in a fresh way that no building here is our greatest joy or our final destination. We gained in our loss.

And then the next loss came:

> *Sarah, we have run out of options. Your ankle will continue to get worse and you may eventually be unable to walk on it. In order to prolong your use of it, you must avoid all running, jumping, and stress on your leg. To the best of your ability, even avoid gaining much weight. In the meantime, we'll make it as comfortable as possible for as long as we can.*

Those were the last words I heard from my orthopedic surgeon. One injury and three intense surgeries later, hope of healing has faded. I'd been an athlete all of my life and found great joy in the ability to play sports, run, and de-stress through physical activity. Now all that has gone, and my future may well include the inability to walk normally.

## Why Would God...?

To be honest, I have felt as though a small part of me has died. In a way, it has. I grieve because I can no longer join friends in pickup volleyball and softball games. I well up when I have to stop myself from running after my children or kicking a soccer ball with them. I battle discouragement as I struggle to find a way to stay healthy when I'm so limited in exercise.

Why would God allow this when he created me with the gift of athleticism and the great pleasure of being active with my children, spouse, and friends? Why would God chop all that out of my life? I have wrestled with the Lord over the many "good" things that he has allowed to be stripped away.

You may well be reading this having lost far more and far better things than I have. You may have had to give up more precious dreams and face worse news than me. You may have much more reason for pain and many more reasons for questioning. Where do we go with that pain and those questions? Well, sometimes answers will be elusive—only God knows fully what his purposes are in the circumstances he allows. But we find some very helpful truth in Jesus' words to his followers the night before he died, hours from his arrest:

> I am the true vine, and my Father is the vinedresser. Every branch in me that does not bear fruit he takes away, and every branch that does bear fruit he prunes, that it may bear more fruit ... I am the vine; you are the branches. Whoever abides in me and I in him, he it is that bears much fruit, for apart from me you can do nothing. (John 15 v 1-2, 5)

God is the Great Gardener—and he prunes the branches of his vine.

Being pruned is a mark of being truly connected to that vine, to Christ. In fact, a branch that is not being pruned is a branch that is not bearing fruit—it is showing by its fruitlessness that it isn't really connected to the vine at all. Beware a life that involves no pruning—it may well suggest that you are not truly in Christ.

On the other hand, if we are in the vine—connected to Christ by faith in him—we will increasingly bear the fruit of Christ-likeness. And part of being fruitful is being pruned. It doesn't take long to realize that the Lord's pruning work is often uncomfortable as we experience the wasting away of our outer selves—as he cuts away at our earthly desires, hopes, expectations, and comforts. So we need to remember Christ's assurance that as we experience these losses—to use Paul's words, as our outer selves waste away—it is always for the purpose of fruitful growth. God is renewing our inner selves day by day.

It's fascinating to me how Christ teaches us truth through something so practical as how a gardener prunes his own garden. Here are some reasons from Garden.com why pruning is beneficial for a plant. These same reasons can easily be connected to the value of God's pruning work in our lives.

## Provoke New Growth

*[Pruning will] improve the plant's overall health—frequently removing older stems encourages a plant to put energy into new growth, thus keeping the plant young.*

As a new creation in Christ, we are being helped to put off our old self and to be renewed in our minds, putting on the new self to reflect more of his image. Sometimes that means something that we want being taken from our lives in order to encourage new growth in areas we wouldn't have sought out on our own.

I didn't choose to have a child with special needs or a family of six with Lyme disease, but God did. While that journey has been so incredibly difficult at times, I can't deny that it has also been the greatest source of sanctifying work in me. By his grace, God has used it to change much of what I value in life—my comforts and wants—transforming me to reflect more of Christ and to accept more of his purposes for me.

 ## Redirect Growth

*[Pruning will] control or direct new growth—each cut will stop the plant's growth in one direction and redirect it in another, guiding the shape and size of the plant.*

When I was in high school, I planned on using the gift of athleticism God had given me to get a scholarship and play sports in college. I worked hard to achieve that plan. But through pain, tears, and confusion, God took that from me and redirected me on a completely new path. That new path led me to the husband I married, the children I now have, and a heart that has increasingly learned the value of surrendering my will to his. God chose to cut away sports from my life so that he could redirect, guide, and shape me for something better.

 ## Prevent Disease

*[Pruning will] prevent the spread of disease—removing dead or damaged branches will decrease the chance of disease entering through dead wood and spreading throughout the plant.*

God's pruning in our lives removes areas that are sin-ridden, including the easy-to-ignore "acceptable" sins, which allows healthier fruit to be produced in us. Better a painful pruning than a dead branch.

## Increase Yield

*[Pruning will] increase the number and quality of fruit, flowers and foliage—pruning at the right time and in the right places can increase*

*the number of shoots produced by the plant, thus increasing yield.*

God uses his word in our lives to convict, teach, train, lead, encourage, and grow us up in Christ. He speaks to us and through us to prune us and increase the fruit produced in our lives. "But those that were sown on the good soil are the ones who hear the word and accept it and bear fruit, thirtyfold and sixtyfold and a hundredfold" (Mark 4 v 20). If we want good fruit to be produced in our lives, we must continually fill ourselves with the word of God.

## Let Light In

*[Pruning will] improve air circulation and allow light to reach inner and lower leaves—it is important to thin dense growth periodically to improve overall shape and health.*

We can become so busy and burdened by the distractions of life that we can barely hear the Holy Spirit speaking to us. The hours we put in at work, the activities we must get our kids to, the many dreams we feel we must fulfill in order to attain happiness, the technology that is always at our fingertips—these things aren't bad things, but they do suck time and energy from us. God's pruning may be necessary in order to turn our attention to things of greater and eternal value. When pruning removes something from us, it often reveals those things that are competing with him for our joy.

## Pruned for a Season

If plants had nerves, I'm sure that their pruning would be painful. To an untrained eye, pruning may even seem harmful to a plant. But the gardener knows that it is necessary, and for the good of the plant. And in God's great wisdom, he knows that when we submit to his pruning, it will be for our good and will produce eternal fruit thirtyfold, sixtyfold, and a hundredfold.

I don't fully understand why God is pruning me as he is. And I wouldn't have chosen it. Some days I question it. Maybe you're in that place today, too. But you and I can trust he knows what he's doing with every pruning cut he makes to us. The Creator knows how to tend to his vine branches. This is what we hang on to. We will be pruned for a season; and we will thrive eternally.

## Reflect

~ In what ways is Christ asking you to submit to his pruning work in your life?
~ Can you see God's grace in areas that didn't seem good at the time, but you now see the growth that has come from them?
~ Are there things that you are not willing to give up, that you think you could not go on without? What would it look like to grow faithful fruit in that area of your life? And are you willing to take a step of faith and ask God to do a pruning work in your life if it is what you truly need?

## Pray

*Lord God, thank you for giving me faith in Christ so that his life might flow into me. Please help me to abide in him today. Father, I am so quick to cling to the things of this world. I fear interruptions of my dreams, comforts, goals, and plans. By your grace, help me to trust that your pruning work in my life is for my own good and not for harm. Please help me to see how I have grown through the ways you have pruned me already; please help me to respond with faith and joy when you next prune me. May I experience the fruit and blessing of your pruning work in my life in order to know more of the joy and hope I have in Christ. Amen.*

*For further meditation:* Ephesians 1 v 11-12; Psalm 138 v 8; Romans 6 v 22

## Journal

_____

_____

_____

_____

_____

_____

_____

_____

_____

_____

_____

_____

_____

_____

_____

_____

_____

_____

_____

_____

_____

_____

### CHAPTER NINETEEN

# Contentment in Crises: A Prayer

"So we do not lose heart. Though our outer self is wasting
away, our inner self is being renewed day by day"

2 CORINTHIANS 4 V 16

*Oh Lord, for years I have prayed for answers, healing, and understanding
in this suffering you have allowed. Yet they have seemed not to come. Many
have prayed to you on our behalf as we have longed for the restoration of
what's been lost. By your grace, we have persevered through trial after trial,
trusting that you would uphold us and bring forth good from all our pain.*

*But many answers we have hoped for haven't come in the ways we desire.
The world's solutions to our pain have left us discouraged, confused, and
fighting hopelessness, while the trials, burdens, questions, and uncertainties
remain the same.*

*Lord, I have longed for, cried, and pleaded for you to bring us out from
under the pain and heaviness of these trials into a place of abundance.
I have asked you to lift these crushing burdens and carry us through the
pounding waves and raging fire that threaten to consume our hope, testi-
mony, and lives.*

*However, I have slowly come to realize that in my desire for answers, I have
missed something far more wonderful. You have answered my prayers—
though in very different ways than I expected. You have been near, intimately working deep within our hearts as we have laid down our hopes and
desires of this world. While you have chosen not to remove the heartache and*

overwhelming circumstances from our lives, you have done something greater. You have brought us into a place of abundance—a place of contentment and freedom, not in the form of the relief that I've been waiting for, but in the midst of the very trials I desired to be freed from.

Lord, I think you've been teaching me that contentment is in the presence of Christ, and not in the absence of pain:

> For you, O God, have tested us;
>   you have tried us as silver is tried.
> You brought us into the net;
>   you laid a crushing burden on our backs;
> you let men ride over our heads;
>   we went through fire and through water;
> yet you have brought us out to a place of abundance.
>
> (Psalm 66 v 10-12)

So much of me wants to fight what you are allowing. My spirit wants to know you deeply and love you more than this world, but at the same time by nature I long for comfort, understanding, and the realization of hopes and desires that I have for my life. But it is by your grace, Father, that you have allowed these trials to continue, and maybe even increase, in order that I would see that your Son alone is where joy, peace, rest, hope, contentment, and satisfaction are found. Though the heartache, loss, and pain are real, the treasures that you are revealing within them are far greater. I know that, even when I don't feel that. So Father, help me press on.

> Come and hear, all you who fear God,
>   and I will tell you what he has done for my soul. (Psalm 66 v 16)

O Lord, my Savior, you have taught me to cling to you with a hope-filled grip. I once loved this world and lived as if it were mine to determine its course, but you loved me enough to take me through the refining fire of affliction. Though the pull of this world is always at work, you have allowed me to experience disappointments, empty hopes, and the loss of temporary comforts in order that my love for the things of this world would fade and my love for you would grow.

*But I often feel so weak. I want to be steadfast and free from the anxiety of my soul and resistance to your will. But much of the time, I'm not. Disappointments still rattle, pain still fogs up the lens of truth, loss still causes deep heartache, and the death of earthly hopes still feels like the death of everything. How can I not lose hope? How can I tell of what you are doing for my inner self instead of lamenting the wasting of my outer self?*

> *You keep him in perfect peace*
>> *whose mind is stayed on you,*
>> *because he trusts in you.*
> *Trust in the LORD forever,*
>> *for the LORD GOD is an everlasting rock. (Isaiah 26 v 3-4)*

*Lord God, you are my everlasting Rock. Help me to live with that in mind. Whether I am in a place of comfort or being tossed by the waves, my peace is found in you. I know I cannot do this apart from you. My mind is too quick to wander and my heart is too quick to doubt. May you keep me in this place of quiet trust and anchor my contentment in you.*

*Oh, how thankful I am for what you have done within my heart. So much of what I feared has become a reality and, yet you haven't wasted a moment of it. You have allowed the loss of my hopes and expectations to open my eyes to how shallow and temporary they really were. As I have died a daily death to my love for the world and desire for comfort, temporary happiness, and control, I have experienced satisfaction and joy by simply resting in your trustworthy presence. You alone have done this.*

*But Lord, you know me. You know I would only be fooling myself if I claimed that fear no longer remains. Fear and anxiety have been close yet unwanted friends. The last 10 years of nearly constant trials have given me every earthly reason to be anxious and afraid. Will my family and I ever be healthy on this side of heaven? Will I ever be able to care for my family with energy and strength in the way that I long to? Will my marriage be able to endure the weight and stress of exhausting daily struggles? Was the choice to walk away from financial comfort worth it? Will we ever be freed from the pain of my son's illness and the ripple effects that it has had within* our family? How long can we carry the financial burdens that continue to come upon us? What's next? What if I reach a breaking point and just can't endure anything more?

> For thus said the Lord GOD, the Holy One of Israel,
> "In returning and rest you shall be saved;
> in quietness and in trust shall be your strength." (Isaiah 30 v 15)

I don't know the answers to these questions. I guess you are teaching me that I don't really need to. I guess I have been learning to look to you to quiet my heart and teach me to rest. I guess you have been teaching me to seek contentment in you now in the trials, rather than assuming it can only lie in my circumstances on the other side of these trials.

Father, help me to stop looking for the light at the end of the tunnel and begin looking for the Light within it. For I know that this place of contentment, a place of true rest and confidence in your presence, is a precious place to be. It frees me from the anxiety of trying to save myself from circumstances that I am not powerful or wise enough to control. It frees me from trying to make sense of the heartache, pain, and loss in this sin-stricken world. And, it frees me from the joy-sucking traps of "what if" and "if only."

Father, please give me the grace to persevere. Help me to accept what you have allowed and rely on your faithful provision, rather than focusing solely on your ability to rescue me from this pain. Some days, I still frantically seek to escape and lose sight of your promises. Quiet my anxious heart and fill me, Jesus, so that I long for nothing other than you. As your servant David said:

> My soul will be satisfied as with fat and rich food,
> and my mouth will praise you with joyful lips,
> when I remember you upon my bed,
> and meditate on you in the watches of the night;
> for you have been my help,
> and in the shadow of your wings I will sing for joy.
> My soul clings to you;
> your right hand upholds me. (Psalm 63 v 5-8)

*Please make me able to say this, and mean it, and experience it. Hide me in the shadow of your wings! When I cannot bear another moment, uphold me with your right hand. This is my prayer—that my soul will be satisfied and I will praise you with joyful lips all the days of my life, even if the pain remains.*

*Lord, you can change my circumstances in a moment if you choose to. You can restore my health, heal my children, free my son from the bondage of his illness, remove the hurt and confusion in my other children, restore the home and income we walked away from, and provide the answers that we pray for. But for now, you have chosen not to. Lord, don't waste a moment of this pain. Instead of letting me fix my eyes solely on my desired outcome and change of circumstances, help me to seek and rest in your provision, guidance, nearness, and heart-changing purposes in the moment and place where you have put me. I trust that it's in this wilderness journey that I will see your faithful provisions and nearness most clearly.*

*Father, I'm longing for the day when I will be in your presence for eternity. But for now, help me find rest in the here and now. You are my place of abundance and, in you, there is contentment, freedom, rest, peace, hope, and joy—even as these waves crash and these fires rage. You are my Rock. Please be my Rock. Thank you. Amen.*

## Reflect

~ If you have been in a long season of suffering, can you see ways that the Lord has grown you and drawn you closer to himself through it?

~ Do you believe it's possible to be content where God has placed you, while still praying for an improvement of circumstances?

~ Do you find satisfaction in knowing Christ or do you need something else to be happy? Do you believe that the Lord knows what you need and is able and willing to provide it?

## Pray

Take a few minutes to write your own prayer to the Lord. Be honest before him with your fears, questions, struggles, sin, doubts, and desires. However, don't end there, but speak truth into your heart and mind by reciting to the Lord his promises, faithfulness, and character. Then ask for his strength to rest and be confident in those truths as you trust your questions and trials to his loving and good plan for you.

*For further meditation:* 2 Corinthians 12 v 10; 1 Timothy 6 v 6-7; Hebrews 13 v 5

# Journal

_____
_____
_____
_____
_____
_____
_____
_____
_____
_____
_____
_____
_____
_____
_____
_____
_____
_____
_____
_____
_____
_____
_____
_____

CHAPTER TWENTY

# Fourteen Reasons to Praise God in the Trials

"So we do not lose heart. Though our outer self is wasting
away, our inner self is being renewed day by day"

2 CORINTHIANS 4 V 16

In a season of terrible difficulty, while living in a city far from home, I
remember wrestling with the Bible's command to rejoice in the Lord
always. At that time, the chronic pain had begun to appear, I had
barely enough money to pay my bills, I was 13 hours from everyone I
loved, and I had no prospects for the future. Any time I would try to
pray, only tears would come.

One day a friend listened to my distress over the phone and gently challenged me: What if, instead of trying to make sense of everything, and
instead of trying desperately to escape my reality, I took seriously God's
command about praising the Lord for who he is and all he had done?

Her suggestion seemed unhelpful. "What would praise do to help
me?" I wondered. Praising the Lord not only seemed unhelpful; it also
felt hypocritical because I was struggling to believe that he was good. I
didn't feel like praising him.

Regardless, I decided that for the next three days I would pursue
praising God aloud or in the silence of my heart, along the lines of his
word. I would seek to give him thanks and worship—even though all I
wanted to do was worry, weep, and doubt.

To my complete surprise, it made a huge difference. While it is hard
to describe the experience, it was like being lifted above the thick and

weighty cloud of my circumstances to see my God more clearly and to cling to his gospel promises more fully. Praising God in suffering is hard. But when we are suffering, praising God is precious. It reminds us that he is far mightier than our hardship, that he reigns and rules over all things, and that he never changes, even when our circumstances do.

Having a praise-filled attitude does not mean that we should never cry out to him in our suffering, or that we should stifle our worries, weeping, and doubts. Praying honestly to God and praising him in suffering are not mutually exclusive actions. This dual reality is scattered throughout Scripture. We need both!

Scripture is saturated with reasons to praise God in trouble. We're going to focus on just one psalm—and 14 springboards for praise that David offers us in Psalm 40.

## 1. God Hears Us

> *I waited patiently for the LORD;*
>   *he inclined to me and heard my cry. (Psalm 40 v 1)*

God is not disinterested or aloof. He is our Father; he is near to us and has brought us near through his Son's death in our place. So he is aware and engaged when his children speak to him.

> *Oh Lord, you have heard my cry! You have not turned your face away from me, but have heard me because I am favored in Jesus.*

## 2. God Rescued Us from Death

> *He drew me up from the pit of destruction,*
>   *out of the miry bog,*
> *and set my feet upon a rock,*
> *making my steps secure. (v 2)*

God has delivered us from the destruction of our souls—an eternity in hell—and has raised us from death to life in Jesus Christ, our immoveable rock of salvation.

*I know that you hear me because you rescued me from damnation! You saved me from the destruction of my soul, and you chose to make me a part of your family, claiming me as your own.*

## 3. God Gives Us Joy and Peace

*He put a new song in my mouth,*
 *a song of praise to our God.*
*Many will see and fear,*
 *and put their trust in the LORD. (v 3)*

The result of what God has done for us in Christ our Lord is cause for thanksgiving, joy, and peace. We always have a song to sing if we trust in the Lord.

*Once I was callous to you, praising the world and all its fading treasures, but now you have given me a new heart and put a new song in my mouth that proclaims your praises.*

## 4. God Satisfies Us

*Blessed is the man who makes the LORD his trust,*
 *who does not turn to the proud,*
*to those who go astray after a lie! (v 4)*

Trouble tempts us to look to ourselves or to the world for help, strength, and hope. But no earthly gift can satisfy these eternal yearnings. Only a limitless God can give us all that we truly need.

*In Christ, I am blessed. I needn't seek my satisfaction in self, worldly gain, or position. I trust in you and you alone to fill me and make me whole.*

167

## 5. God Cares for Us

*You have multiplied, O LORD my God,*
  *your wondrous deeds and your thoughts toward us;*
*none can compare with you!*
  *I will proclaim and tell of them,*
*yet they are more than can be told. (v 5)*

God is mighty, awesome, and infinite; we are weak, sinful, and temporal. It is stunning that such a glorious God would care for us—and in such an abundant way!

*Awesome God, none can compare with you! Who am I, Lord, that you would be mindful of me, caring for me and working for my good? I deserve nothing, for my life is wasting away, but you have given me an abundance in yourself.*

 ## 6. God Has Made Us Righteous

*In sacrifice and offering you have not delighted,*
  *but you have given me an open ear.*
*Burnt offering and sin offering you have not required. (v 6)*

Jesus became sin for us, that we would become his righteousness. God does not require a sin offering from us because he became the sin offering for us.

*I praise you for making me righteous in Jesus, apart from anything that I have done! Thank you that your Son was willing to bear my sin on the cross.*

## 7. God Gave Us a New Heart

*Then I said, "Behold, I have come;*
  *in the scroll of the book it is written of me:*

*I delight to do your will, O my God;*
  *your law is within my heart." (v 7-8)*

Where once we hated God's law and could not obey it, now he has given us the desire and the power to do his will. His law has been written on our new hearts of flesh by his Holy Spirit.

*God, you have given me a new heart that is sensitive to you and fears you. Now your word and ways are my delight!*

## 8. God Has Made Us Gospel Heralds

*I have told the glad news of deliverance*
  *in the great congregation;*
*behold, I have not restrained my lips,*
  *as you know, O LORD. (v 9)*

We now have good news to share with others; both those who need to grow in appreciation of the gospel and those who as yet have no appreciation of the gospel.

*Thank you that you give me the privilege of working powerfully in others, for their good, by sharing with them the powerful gospel.*

## 9. God's Faithful Love Never Changes

*I have not hidden your deliverance within my heart;*
  *I have spoken of your faithfulness and your salvation;*
*I have not concealed your steadfast love and your faithfulness*
  *from the great congregation. (v 10)*

God has saved us because he first loved us and set that love upon us in unending faithfulness through salvation. Our deliverance was not God's duty, but his delight!

*You are faithful and your love is steadfast! It is your faithfulness and love that drove you to save me. You rescued me because you delighted in me.*

## 10. God Is Merciful

*As for you, O LORD, you will not restrain*
*    your mercy from me;*
*your steadfast love and your faithfulness will*
*    ever preserve me! (v 11)*

What God began in our salvation, he promises to complete. By his mercy, even when we sin, he will keep us in his love for now unto eternity.

*Awesome God, your mercy is wonderful, and it covers my sin. You preserve my faith, even though I wrestle with despair, self-pity, pride, discontentment, and bitterness.*

## 11. God Keeps Us Close

*For evils have encompassed me*
*    beyond number;*
*my iniquities have overtaken me,*
*    and I cannot see;*
*they are more than the hairs of my head;*
*    my heart fails me. (v 12)*

It is good when our hearts fail us, for then we remember that only our unfailing God can sustain us, strengthen us, and provide for our every need.

*Sometimes my troubles and sin seem too much for me to bear, but it is good when my heart fails me; for then I see my need for you more clearly. Thank you, Lord!*

## 12. God Is the Perfect Judge

*Be pleased, O LORD, to deliver me!*
*O LORD, make haste to help me!*
*Let those be put to shame and disappointed altogether*
*who seek to snatch away my life;*
*let those be turned back and brought to dishonor*
*who delight in my hurt!*
*Let those be appalled because of their shame*
*who say to me, "Aha, Aha!" (v 13-15)*

What a comfort that the just judge of all the earth is also the Savior of sinners! We can entrust our troubles to him because he judges justly and will do what is right.

*You fight for me, O Lord Jesus, and you deliver me from the enemy of my soul. You have brought the evil one to dishonor and shame by defeating death, and one day you will put him away forever.*

## 13. God Is the Source of Joy

*But may all who seek you*
*rejoice and be glad in you;*
*may those who love your salvation*
*say continually, "Great is the LORD!" (v 16)*

Gladness is found in him, not in our willpower to be glad or to make good of our troubles. We are able to rejoice because the Lord is great, and because he has satisfied our greatest eternal yearning through salvation.

*I rejoice in who you are! You have given me more in yourself than I could ever want or need. You say that if I seek you, I will find you, because you have first loved me.*

## 14. God Will Help Us

*As for me, I am poor and needy,*
*but the Lord takes thought for me.*
*You are my help and my deliverer;*
*do not delay, O my God! (v 17)*

God's deliverance is not only for our past sins and our future eternity; his deliverance is for our present need. His Spirit is always with us and for us, to help us through trouble.

*I really am poor and needy. But you care, O Lord. Do not delay to make good of this suffering and, one day, to end it completely. Help, God! Come, Lord Jesus!*

## Cause to Praise

Praise is possible in the darkness. And it is as we praise God that he renews our inner self. To fuel your praise, the best thing to do is to ask God for his help, and then open his word and start reading. You will find cause to praise him before long!

## Reflect

If you have not done so already (and even if you have!), you could work through the fourteen short prayers above, making these prayers your own in praise of God.

# Pray

*Lord Almighty, I do want to praise you! I do want to turn my mind to all you are, and what you have done! Help me. Lift my gaze above the weightiness of my circumstances, that praise would be on my lips. Give me power and strength to fix my eyes on you. You are worthy, Lord, of all my praise, and I know I do not praise you as I should. But I want to, I really want to. I do love you, Lord. Amen.*

*For further meditation:* Psalm 107; Psalm 145

*Journal*

CHAPTER TWENTY-ONE

Living for the Unseen

"For this light momentary affliction is preparing for us an eternal weight of glory beyond all comparison, as we look not to the things that are seen but to the things that are unseen"

2 CORINTHIANS 4 V 17-18

Recently I asked three of my kids what they pictured when they thought of heaven. My 7-year-old responded, "I'm pretty sure there will be gold streets and cupcakes. Lots of cupcakes." (To be fair, he can't eat gluten, dairy, or corn, so I can't blame him for longing for cupcakes.)

My 5-year-old thought hard and responded, "I'm not really sure, but I'm pretty positive that there will be boats and beaches." (I think she's associated heaven a little bit with Florida, but at least she's picturing something beautiful.)

My 3-year-old simply looked at me with a confused expression and said, "Huh?"

I remember having similar thoughts about heaven as a young child. I pictured a place where we enjoyed our favorite things, floated in the sky, and joined the choir of angels. Sure, it sounded great (unless you can't sing), but to be honest, the tangible things of earth were far more enticing.

## *Is Your Heaven Bland?*

So much of what we struggle with in this life is magnified when we have this kind of bland view of our future. This lackluster idea of eternity makes our lives feel far more important and our sufferings seem all-consuming, disastrous and pointless. We become consumed with focusing on the moment at hand, planning, dreaming, and working toward our goals. We seek satisfaction through our talents, successes, relationships, and outward morality, ultimately causing us either to settle for contentment in the temporal pleasures of this world or else become miserable and hopeless when life doesn't pan out as we expected it to.

Our view of eternity changes everything here. If we are to know joy in our trials now, we need to begin to be excited about the "eternal weight of glory" that is coming. And that single phrase that Paul chooses to use to describe eternity with Christ should be enough to fuel that excitement.

## *Eternal*

Do you ever stop to think about the incredible realities of eternal life? Every day there's a tomorrow, and that tomorrow will never bring disappointment or death. There will be no fear of the future or striving to keep what can be lost. There will only be joy in knowing that tomorrow is just as secure as today.

I find it hard to fathom. All you and I have ever known is the uncertainty of what tomorrow may bring and the realities of unmet expectations, circumstances that we can't make sense of, fighting against failing bodies, and knowing that we will one day lose those that we love. Everything on this earth has an expiration date—except for our souls. But one day, our struggle and striving will end. Our uncertainties and our mortality will be no more. For those in Christ, eternity with our Savior will be all the more sweet after tasting the bitterness of this earth. Fix your eyes on your promised eternity. It gives perspective to your present. This life is a blink compared to the eternity of eternity! It may not feel like it right now, but it is "momentary," and so are its troubles.

# Glorious

*God's glory is the radiance of his holiness, the radiance of his manifold, infinitely worthy and valuable perfections. (John Piper, desiringgod. org/interviews/what-is-gods-glory)*

Apart from the cleansing blood of Christ, we could never stand before God's pure holiness and infinite perfection—his glory. This is why to God's Old Testament people, the thought of God's glory was incredibly attractive, and yet utterly terrifying, and impossible for any of God's people to fully see and live. Even Moses, perhaps the greatest of all of God's Old Testament people, could survive only a glimpse:

> And the LORD said to Moses, "This very thing that you have spoken I will do, for you have found favor in my sight, and I know you by name." Moses said, "Please show me your glory." And he said, "I will make all my goodness pass before you and will proclaim before you my name 'The LORD.' And I will be gracious to whom I will be gracious, and will show mercy on whom I will show mercy. But," he said, "you cannot see my face, for man shall not see me and live." And the LORD said, "Behold, there is a place by me where you shall stand on the rock, and while my glory passes by I will put you in a cleft of the rock, and I will cover you with my hand until I have passed by. Then I will take away my hand, and you shall see my back, but my face shall not be seen." (Exodus 33 v 17-23)

Moses desired to see God's glory, and yet he could not bear the full magnitude of it. As with looking into the sun, he could survive a glimpse but would have been blinded—struck dead, in fact—by its fullness.

But eternity is "glorious." It will be full of the dazzling light of God's glory—and, forgiven and purified by the Son and made finally perfect by the Spirit, you will enter the gates of heaven, and enjoy gazing at that glory! Can you imagine being with God and living with him face to face without fear? The God of the universe, who spoke creation into existence, intimately created you and me, and sustains all things will be living among us. We will be able to touch him, see him, talk with him, and worship him without shame, sin, or fear. Our faith will finally become sight and we will enter into the indescribable glory of God and the precious presence of Christ—the place we were made for. What a glorious, eternal future we have awaiting us!

## Beyond All Comparison

Our future is eternal and glorious, and so it is beyond all comparison with our present. This weight of glory is far greater in value and worth than anything we may experience in this life—both our greatest joys and deepest sorrows. We press on in our sufferings because they are all a part of "preparing for us" this eternal weight of glory beyond all comparison. We can—we should—excitedly long for the day when we can each look back and, informed not by faith but by sight, say, "Paul was right! Nothing—no pleasure or pain in that momentary time I had before I arrived here—can compare to being at home with my Savior, living in the fullness of being all that God created me to be, and basking in his eternal presence and glory."

## Seeing Eternity Changes How We See Suffering

Of course, today our suffering feels very far from light and very far from momentary. In our limited earthly vision, much of suffering feels heavy, all-encompassing, and never-ending. However, in this lies the treasure of God's grace through suffering. Not only is suffering one of God's greatest tools for transforming us into people who are more and more like Christ, but it wakes us up to the pain of sin and stirs in our hearts a desire for something greater, something lasting. In God's grace, he uses our suffering to point us forward so that we don't settle for now, but seize the hope of our future. These graces in disguise begin to loosen our grip on the comfortable life we so desperately seek to hold on to, replacing it with the life-giving hope of the gospel.

So, today, "look not to the things that are seen but to the things that are unseen." When you are struggling to look past your immediate circumstances, remember the three promises that we have in this single phrase describing our future: Eternal. Glorious. Beyond all comparison. Recite these words to yourself and ask the Lord to grow your vision of eternity in order that the ups and downs of this life would shrink in comparison to your glorious future.

Eternal. Glorious. Beyond all comparison. That's a future better even than cupcakes and beaches!

## Reflect

~ When you think of heaven, what comes to mind? Do you long for heaven simply for relief of pain or has Christ increased in you a desire to be with him above anything else?

~ Have you found suffering to increase your longing for things of eternal value or has it created a hardness and bitterness within your heart? Would you ask Christ to soften your heart and open your eyes to the unequaled treasure of eternal life with him?

~ If you are a Christian, how would the way you see your circumstances change if you began to look at them through the lens of your promised future—eternal, glorious, and beyond all comparison?

## Pray

*Heavenly Father, some days the suffering in my life feels as if it's too much to bear. I struggle to see past the pain and heartache that so often seems to come my way. And I find it hard to believe these troubles are light or momentary. They don't feel that way, Father. Please show me the future you have prepared for me, and that I will reach as I walk forward with faith in your Son. Please give me a greater vision of life in your eternal, glorious, incomparable presence. Please would that change my perspective on my trials and my joys today. Give me your strength, Lord, to see beyond the moment and rest in the hope of eternity today. Amen.*

*For further meditation:* Psalm 25 v 8-9; Luke 18 v 29-30; Revelation 22 v 4-7

*Journal*

_____

_____

_____

_____

_____

_____

_____

_____

_____

_____

_____

_____

_____

_____

_____

_____

_____

_____

_____

_____

_____

_____

## CHAPTER TWENTY-TWO

Not There
Yet

"We look not to the things that are seen but to the things that
are unseen. For the things that are seen are transient, but the
things that are unseen are eternal"

2 CORINTHIANS 4 V 18

We know where we are headed. We have ahead of us an
inheritance sharing an eternal weight of glory. One day, what is
now unseen will be seen and will finally be ours by sight, when
faith disappears and the old world—what we can see now—passes
away.

But not yet. For believers living in the realm of "things-seen-now,"
distractions are everywhere, sin often runs rampant, and evil seems to
have the upper hand. Our affections for Jesus are fickle, as is our hunger
for hearing from him and speaking to him. More urgent, pleasurable,
self-serving realities steal our attention, so we look to worldly gain and
immediate comfort... and desire them. At the same time, we see violence, injustice, and suffering... and we fear them.

Our earthly afflictions point each of us to the deeper problem which,
in Peter's words, "wage[s] war against your soul" (1 Peter 2 v 11). Suffering often acts as a magnifying glass to the "passions of the flesh," or
selfish desires within us. In affliction, we can see our sin more clearly
because suffering exposes our pride, anger, selfishness, and shame.
Yet in another sense, suffering blinds us to sin because we have a
ready-made excuse for giving in to our selfish passions, and we can

kid ourselves that, if only our pain were removed, we would behave in a more God-honoring way.

Kari is a dear friend of mine who has struggled through the hardship of sudden hearing loss. I once heard her say, "Sinfulness will always be my greatest earthly struggle." That is a shocking statement, coming from a woman who can no longer hear without aid. How can she say this?!

But Kari couldn't be more right. She is looking through what she can now see into the realm of things unseen. She knows there is a war being waged within her heart, a battle against sin that she must fight by looking to her unseen Lord and Savior, as she walks on by faith toward the unseen eternal future he has won for her. Suffering will not stop her getting there. But sin could, if it blooms into unbelief.

If sin is real and these realities are true, then how do we look to the things that are unseen? How do we keep our eyes fixed on Jesus Christ in this broken, sinful world?

Peter addresses these questions in his first letter to suffering Christian churches who are being mocked, maligned and more for their faith. He urges them to look to their unseen Lord, in a time of increasing pressure and persecution from the things-seen-now world.

> *Therefore, preparing your minds for action, and being sober-minded, set your hope fully on the grace that will be brought to you at the revelation of Jesus Christ. As obedient children, do not be conformed to the passions of your former ignorance, but as he who called you is holy, you also be holy in all your conduct, since it is written, "You shall be holy, for I am holy." (1 Peter 1 v 13-16)*

## Think About Who Is Coming...

Your mind is a powerful and influential gift from God. This is why Peter addresses the subject of the mind in looking to things unseen. He uses the phrase "gird up the loins of your mind." Picture a first-century man dressed in a long tunic, tucking the fabric tails into his belt as he heads into battle. That is what we are to do. We are to have minds ready to think clearly about what we cannot see.

Our pastor, Colin Smith, memorably puts it like this: "Whatever grips the mind controls the heart." How we think, and what we think about, will be integral to the way that we live. Like Peter's first readers, we are Christians in the world of things-seen-now, living away from our final home and engaged in a spiritual fight. We, too, need to think about where we are headed and to whom we belong. If we do not think about these truths, we will not live as if this is true.

Here is what Peter wants us to think about:

~ We have a heavenly inheritance that is imperishable, undefiled, and unfading, kept for us by God himself (v 4).
~ Until then, trials are good because they test the genuineness of our faith and show us the faithfulness of Christ to sustain us (v 7).
~ God has caused us to love and believe and rejoice in his Son, even though we can't see him; and he will keep us in this love until we do see him (v 8-9).

Peter says, *Look to what is coming! All this is yours in Jesus!* We process the world of things-seen-now by thinking about these unseen realities. We get clear on what's important and eternal in our present by preparing our minds with a focus on the inheritance of our future. We set our hope fully—not partially or half-heartedly—on the grace that will be brought when Christ comes. We look to him by setting our minds on his truth.

## Now Live in Light of Your Hope

Whatever grips the mind controls the heart—and directs the body. "As he who called you is holy, you also be holy in all your conduct" (v 15). Godly obedience flows from God's calling, Peter says. A mind saturated in gospel truths will be a heart compelled to live in light of them, rather than being directed by what's right in front of us. God's calling produces obedient children who desire to live for things unseen:

*And if you call on him as Father who judges impartially according to each one's deeds, conduct yourselves with fear throughout the time of your exile, knowing that you were ransomed from the futile ways inherited from your forefathers. (v 17-18)*

Two unseen realities produce holiness in us. The first is our heavenly inheritance in Christ, and the hope we have set fully in him as we wait to see him. The second is that God will be our impartial Judge, to whom we will give an account for every moment we spent on earth; and so we must live in awe of him now.

The fear of the Lord means that we worship him for who he is, not some domesticated shrunk-down version that we're more comfortable with, but who does not exist and cannot save. God is not a house cat, he is a lion—and while you may love a house cat, you fear a lion. You live in awe of its power, even as you admire its beauty.

So if we fear the unseen God, we will honor and consider him—his power, lordship, and authority—in everything we think and say and do. This is a love-and-awe-motivated fear that results in holiness now and an even fuller hope in what's to come.

The "Father who judges" is a reality that we as Christians don't often think about. Yes, we are secure in Christ, righteous in God's sight, and no longer condemned because of Christ's precious blood. But we will be judged in the sense that our earthly deeds will not be without importance. Our obedience will be brought to light. So will our lack of obedience. We will have to give an account for what we did with our lives and how we responded to our circumstances—including our suffering.

"Sinfulness will always be my greatest earthly struggle." So think about what, and who is coming... and live in light of that unseen hope. Look around you. What you see right now will pass away. But the One who gives you grace and hope never will.

# Reflect

~ What do you think about most often? How do you think these thought-patterns affect your heart and, therefore, your actions?

~ What are some practical ways you can prepare your mind for action in this sinful, broken world?

~ What does God's grace mean for you in times of disobedience, or when you've desired earthly things over eternal ones? Apply his gospel grace to your sin, and praise him for his forgiveness and love in Christ!

# Pray

*Heavenly Father, you are worthy to be praised, worthy to be loved and feared! Please help me to set my hope fully on all you have given me, by thinking about what is true and about who you are. Make me increasingly holy, and help me fear you in the way I live. I acknowledge that my greatest struggle will always be my sinfulness. Thank you for saving me from my sin, and changing me to hate that sin, and leading me to the place where there is no sin. Help me to love you, even though I do not yet see you, and to look to the things that are unseen until I am face to face with you. In Jesus' name, Amen.*

*For further meditation:* Psalm 16; Matthew 5 v 29-30; Philippians 4 v 8-9

# *Journal*

# CHAPTER TWENTY-THREE

# A House Not Made With Hands

"For we know that if the tent that is our earthly home is destroyed, we have a building from God, a house not made with hands, eternal in the heavens. For in this tent we groan, longing to put on our heavenly dwelling, if indeed by putting it on we may not be found naked. For while we are still in this tent, we groan, being burdened—not that we would be unclothed, but that we would be further clothed, so that what is mortal may be swallowed up by life"

2 CORINTHIANS 5 V 1-4

*O*n the days when my body is rebelling because the chronic pain has returned, I literally groan.

I cry out through words, or I cry out through tears, as I lose heart over my weakness. Usually, this groaning issues from disappointment, fear, grumbling, and sadness over being laid up on the couch—again. Over canceled plans—again. Over the healthy, strong body I used to have. Groaning can become an end in itself, a wordless expression of a weary body.

But there is another, better, way to groan. In these wonderful verses, Paul tells me that my groaning can also be the overflow of the expectation of a forward-looking heart. This is groaning with a different perspective. We groan when our bodies, minds, and hearts are hurting, yes, but do we understand the deeper reality this groaning points to? There is more to our groaning than meets the eye.

187

## What Your Groans Are Saying

Whether we realize it or not, when "in this tent we groan" it is because deep down we are "longing to put on our heavenly dwelling." Our earthly groaning is evidence that we were created for another world, a trouble-free existence where our bodies work, our hearts love, and our minds are clear. The aching in our bodies now does not need to be an end in itself but an indicator of new beginnings. We groan for peace, restoration, healing, and wholeness, which is good and right and full of hope—if we allow our groans to point us forward. Believer, your groaning points to life with Christ, when the battle against sin has been won, when relationships with other believers have been reconciled from conflict and confusion, when diseases and pain are healed, and when creation-order is restored.

You have a new body to look forward to, "a building from God, a house not made with hands, eternal in the heavens." This final dwelling is the new body that Christ will give us in place of our earthly tents when he returns to usher in the new heaven and earth, and his people are raised bodily.

We need to have a Bible-soaked picture of where we are heading. Books and movies about heaven can so often be deceiving, making us think that heaven is a mysterious, light-filled place where we all turn into floating spirits. But the Bible tells us something different and far more exciting: heaven will be real as real can be, with renewed bodies, renewed minds, renewed relationships, and renewed purpose—the clothing of the truest life possible in the presence of Jesus. It will be heaven on earth: a physical, embodied existence.

## Indestructible

In our heavenly bodies, we will be indestructible. Paul was a tentmaker by trade (Acts 18 v 3), and he compares our earthly bodies to the destructible nature of a fabric tent. Think about the last time you went camping. You weren't counting on your tent to last forever. Rather, you put stakes in the ground for a time, knowing that the tent would get deconstructed whenever the trip was over. Maybe nature threatened to pull down your tent before you felt it was time. Gale-force winds rip up pegs, water seeps into the fabric seams, and predators trespass. Tents are easily disturbed and destroyed.

Like tents, our bodies are destructible. We get sick and injured, and even if we avoid major calamities throughout the course of our lives, we will age and we will die. The journey toward death is inevitable, and every day that we breathe is one day closer to the end of our earthly bodies.

But in our heavenly dwelling, Paul tells us that we will gain new bodies that cannot be destroyed. No outside forces will assail us, whether sickness, natural disaster, or time. We will be stronger than the strongest human being who ever lived, and we will finally be free from all the natural, physical effects of sin. Cancer, bereavement, mental instability, financial insecurity... These forces of nature will never again rip up your tent pegs, because you will be a firmly established building. Chronic pain, regret, childlessness... the seepage of these perpetual disappointments will be no longer. Heartbreak, abuse... your heavenly building will be free of all intruders and predators.

No longer destructible tents, we will be immoveable, firm buildings from God, eternal in the heavens. Your heavenly dwelling will be like a solid building on a firm foundation, unshakeable and made to last.

## Eternal

In our heavenly bodies, we will live forever. In our earthly tents, time is fast fleeing away. We either want more time, pining for wrinkle reducers and face lifts, or we yearn for the end of it, along with the removal of our pain.

Yet, the closer we get to physical death—as far away as that day may feel, and as scary as it may seem—the nearer we get to finally living with Christ in the timelessness of a new, eternal body. One day life will be forever, and forever will be good news. Earthly death becomes everlasting life for believers! At last, our physical state will match the state of our souls, which have been purchased by Christ. You will live forever, and you will love to live.

## Perfect

In our heavenly bodies, we will be robed in righteousness. At the day of the Lord, Jesus Christ will return to claim all who are his, and he will finally clothe us with our indestructible, eternal bodies. Until Christ comes, believers who have gone to be with the Lord await the full clothing of their heavenly dwelling. At the day of the Lord, believers will be with all the saints who have gone before them.

Paul says that we will not be found naked on that day. He means that we will not be ashamed as we stand before Christ our Lord, because he will have dressed us with his sinless perfection, his clean and pure holiness. Every sin, struggle, and suffering that we dealt with on earth will be washed away by the precious blood of the Son, and we will be "further clothed" in a splendid array of his righteousness. What freedom, what joy to finally be enveloped by perfection!

## Face to Face

Best of all, in our heavenly dwelling we will finally see Christ. My breath is taken away at the thought of this remarkable reality. Though we love him now, we cannot see him now. But, robed physically in our resurrection bodies, we will see him and know him fully, even as we are fully known by him. Robed spiritually in the indestructible and eternal righteousness of the Lamb, we will worship him forever. All of the benefits of heaven will be wonderful to us, yes, but none so glorious as Christ himself. He is our greatest delight and our highest reward!

## How Will You Groan?

Your groaning need not be, and should not be, an end in itself, but a forward-looking and forward-leaning hope in what and Who is coming. Your suffering says that something is not right, that there should be more; the gospel confirms that, wonderfully, there is more. There is a coming of Christ to look forward to and there is a heavenly body to anticipate. Don't waste your groaning. It is a cry for a better future. It is a cry that Christ answers. This mortal body is just your tent. One day, you will have a body that is your home, forever, and you will be home, with Jesus.

## Reflect

~ How does the reality that your groaning testifies to your heavenly dwelling encourage you today? How can you use your groaning to point you forward to Christ?
~ Who needs to hear about this future reality today?
~ Which of these realities is hardest for you to grasp? Who could you ask to pray for you and speak with you about it, to keep reminding you that it is true, and that by faith it is yours?

## Pray

*O Lord Jesus, come! I await you. I long to be made whole in your presence, but mostly to finally be with you. To worship you in your presence at last will be my greatest joy, and I need you to help me remember this reality when I'm hurting. Please help me as I groan to groan well. Please would my groans remind me that this body is not my final body. Please would my groans be mixed with joy at the prospect of that heavenly body. Please keep me excited about where I am heading and the greatest joy of that place—seeing you face to face. Amen.*

*For further meditation:* Revelation 1; Revelation 19; 1 Thessalonians 4 v 13-18

## Journal

## CHAPTER TWENTY-FOUR

# Invest Your Groans

"For we know that if the tent that is our earthly home is destroyed, we have a building from God, a house not made with hands, eternal in the heavens. For in this tent we groan, longing to put on our heavenly dwelling, if indeed by putting it on we may not be found naked. For while we are still in this tent, we groan, being burdened—not that we would be unclothed, but that we would be further clothed, so that what is mortal may be swallowed up by life"

2 CORINTHIANS 5 V 1-4

*D*isoriented. Numb. Somber. There are few words to describe where my heart has been lately. I feel inadequate to describe all the reasons why or how I have gotten to this place but, even if I were able adequately to describe them, the circumstances aren't the point. The point is that being a Christian does not exempt me, or anyone else, from desperation and despair. I've found myself in a place that I've never been before.

Maybe it's a physical survival response, or maybe it's an escape mechanism. Either way, I've found myself detached, struggling to find my way out of the darkness. I have always been a fighter, for better or worse. However, it's a scary place when you feel your fight begin to fade and your resolve begin to weaken. I find it useless to carry a façade of strength when all I feel is weak. What do I do with the groaning within my soul?

Thankfully, God's word gives us permission to groan like this. It's not a stranger to this kind of experience. Witness, for instance, David and Job, two heroes of the Bible who nevertheless experienced seasons of despair and hopelessness.

> *TO THE CHOIRMASTER. A PSALM OF DAVID.*
> *Be gracious to me, O LORD, for I am in distress;*
> *my eye is wasted from grief;*
> *my soul and my body also.*
> *For my life is spent with sorrow,*
> *and my years with sighing;*
> *my strength fails because of my iniquity,*
> *and my bones waste away. (Psalm 31 Inscription, v 9-10)*

> *Like a slave who longs for the shadow,*
> *and like a hired hand who looks for his wages,*
> *so I am allotted months of emptiness,*
> *and nights of misery are apportioned to me ...*
> *Therefore I will not restrain my mouth;*
> *I will speak in the anguish of my spirit;*
> *I will complain in the bitterness of my soul. (Job 7 v 2-3, 11)*

Their struggles reassure us that despairing groans are not a sign that we're outside of God's purposes or beyond his reach. I'm so thankful that we can bring all this before the Lord honestly, unafraid of being cast aside.

Scripture, however, doesn't leave us with only groaning (as we saw in the previous chapter)—it moves us on from it. How? By reminding us of three core truths of which God reminded Israel, his people, through their leader Moses, as they traveled through the wilderness toward his promised land. In fact, God's people have always needed to be told, repeatedly, to remember because, repeatedly, we forget. Israel didn't (and we don't) need to learn something new and innovative; we need to remember these basic and unchanging truths.

## Remember... His Past Faithfulness

*And you shall remember the whole way that the LORD your God has led you these forty years in the wilderness ... Your clothing did not wear out on you and your foot did not swell these forty years. Know then in your heart that, as a man disciplines his son, the LORD your God disciplines you. (Deuteronomy 8 v 2a, 4-5)*

When everything seems foggy and we can't make sense of our circumstances or emotions, we have to remember God's past faithfulness. Suffering has a way of sending us into a tailspin of misery and self-pity, causing us to forget how faithful God has been and will continue to be. Therefore, while it's more comfortable to sit and wallow in our pain, we have to drench ourselves in remembering ways he has been faithful to us in the past, as well as evidence of his continual faithfulness through Scripture and, most importantly, the gospel.

When you feel God may not come through for you in a season of difficulty, remember that he has always come through for you in the past, most gloriously at the cross.

## Remember... His Love and Purpose

*... that he might humble you, testing you to know what was in your heart, whether you would keep his commandments or not. And he humbled you and let you hunger and fed you with manna, which you did not know, nor did your fathers know, that he might make you know that man does not live by bread alone, but man lives by every word that comes from the mouth of the LORD. ... So you shall keep the commandments of the LORD your God by walking in his ways and by fearing him.*
*(Deuteronomy 8 v 2b-3, 6)*

Often, we may not fully understand or see the ways God is working in our lives, but we need to remember that the love he has for us drove him to sacrifice his own Son for our freedom. That same love will only allow circumstances that will bring forth greater life in us if we trust him.

Right now, although I feel almost crippled by my daily struggles and looming future, I am strengthened by the truth that God allowed the Israelites to hunger in order to provide for them in ways that only he could. If nothing else, I am learning that we do not live by bread alone—that the physical is not all there is and is never enough. When we are humbled and completely dependent on the Lord in the wilderness, it teaches us to remember, even in times of comfort and abundance, that it is God's faithfulness and power, and not our own strength or wisdom, that we most need. Remember that your trials are never without purpose; your emotions and confusion are never without purpose. All are sent from the One who uses everything to draw his children closer to him and keep them walking toward the promised land of his presence.

 *Remember... His Promises About Your Future*

*For the LORD your God is bringing you into a good land, a land of brooks of water, of fountains and springs, flowing out in the valleys and hills ... And you shall eat and be full, and you shall bless the LORD your God for the good land he has given you.*

*(Deuteronomy 8 v 7, 10)*

This suffering will not last forever. By God's grace, you may see some level of redemption—some freeing from the pain—in your suffering during this lifetime; but whether you do or not, remember that all will be redeemed one day. The confusion, battle, sadness, loss, and disappointment will one day be washed away in the precious sight of eternity with Christ. Whatever good things you have gone without now—whatever precious things you have cried about now—you will be "full" of them in God's good land. When the "mortal [is] swallowed up by life," your wilderness will become a land of plenty and, oh how precious it will be in contrast to this broken world.

## Speak to Your Groans

These were the truths that David and Job, in different times and facing different sets of difficult circumstances, clung to, to keep from losing all hope and giving way to complete despair in their groaning. They remembered. They remembered God's past faithfulness, purposes in their pain, anchoring promises, and future hope.

> *My God, my God, why have you forsaken me?*
> *Why are you so far from saving me, from the words of my groaning?*
> *O my God, I cry by day, but you do not answer,*
> *and by night, but I find no rest.*
> *Yet you are holy,*
> *enthroned on the praises of Israel.*
> *In you our fathers trusted;*
> *they trusted, and you delivered them.*
> *To you they cried and were rescued;*
> *in you they trusted and were not put to shame...*
> *For he has not despised or abhorred*
> *the affliction of the afflicted,*
> *and he has not hidden his face from him,*
> *but has heard, when he cried to him.* (Psalm 22 v 1-5, 24)

> *For I know that my Redeemer lives,*
> *and at the last he will stand upon the earth.*
> *And after my skin has been thus destroyed,*
> *yet in my flesh I shall see God,*
> *whom I shall see for myself,*
> *and my eyes shall behold, and not another.*
> *My heart faints within me!* (Job 19 v 25-27)

And so, I too am learning to remember these truths. When the noise in my head is disorienting, my flesh is wanting to escape and numb the pain, the trials in front of me are suffocating, and the future looks too daunting, I must remember these truths.

I do not know how God will carry me through and what the outcome of the days to come will be. I do not know what tomorrow will bring, or exactly how I'll walk through it. But I will fix my eyes with confidence on my eternal hope and faithful Savior. I will walk forward knowing that one day, maybe very soon, "what is mortal [will] be swallowed up by life."

Until then, I groan. And I remember.

## Reflect

~ Are you willing to bring yourself honestly before the Lord, even with your doubts, questions, and fears?

~ Which of these three commands to remember have been easiest for you to forget?

~ How can remembering these truths impact the way you view your circumstances? Will you take time right now to come to the Lord with your whole heart, asking him to help you remember his promises within your trials?

## Pray

*Lord, thank you for providing examples of biblical heroes who groaned honestly in their afflictions, but also showed me how to fight against hopelessness within. You know the circumstances I face and how easily they can tempt me to despair. Father, help me remember how you have been faithful in the past when I struggle to see your faithfulness in the moment. Help me remember that you use trials to reveal to me your love and teach me to cling to you. And Lord, when I see no earthly hope to hold on to, help me remember the glory and fullness of the land you have called me to and are leading me to. Forgive me for my quickness to forget, and help me to rest secure in remembering all that you have promised. Amen.*

*For further meditation:* Deuteronomy 6 v 20-23; John 14 v 26; 2 Timothy 2 v 8

## Journal

CHAPTER TWENTY-FIVE

# He Has Given Us the Spirit

"He who has prepared us for this very thing is God, who has given us the Spirit as a guarantee"

2 CORINTHIANS 5 V 5

God always makes good on his promises. Always! He has promised that we will be swallowed up by resurrection life on the day we see Jesus face to face, and we know this promise is good because he's given to us his Holy Spirit.

Paul uses the word "guarantee" to describe the significance of this gift. What a forward-looking, faith-filled word this is! We do not yet see with our eyes what God has prepared for his people, but with the eyes of faith we wait for him to reveal it. We wait for him to complete the spiritual transaction he began when he redeemed us by Jesus' costly blood on the cross. By giving us his Holy Spirit, God is saying, *I guarantee that I will make good on the promise to bring you home to me. I will finish what I started. You are mine.* The Holy Spirit is the down-payment—our guarantee that God will complete the purchase and bring us home to be with him forever.

We should not think, however, that God's giving of his Spirit is a type of divine "IOU," where God hands us a marker for his guarantee and then disappears until that day (like when you order your food at the counter, get the marker, and then wait at your table for it to arrive). No, the Holy Spirit is God, his very life and love and presence—his very self—come to dwell within us. The Spirit is the third person of the Trinity, equal in "God-ness" to God the Father and Jesus the Son, and yet distinct in his role. What is that role? To reveal God's presence to us, in order to sustain and strengthen our faith. The Spirit first enables us to grasp the gospel, as he welcomes us into the family of God through faith in Christ. He then shapes us with the gospel, as we wait to be with Christ.

Our current time of struggle, hardship and groaning is also full of God's active presence; we are not left alone while we press on toward all that God has prepared for us, but are able to look to, depend upon and be guided by his Holy Spirit. He helps us walk by faith now by his presence until we have full spiritual sight in his presence.

What are some specific ways that the Holy Spirit helps us walk by faith? Let's turn to Romans 8, where Paul gives us four marks of the Spirit's ministry within believers:

## Reassurance of Life

In this time of waiting and groaning, the presence of sin and the brokenness of suffering discourage us and may even tempt us to despair, making it easy for us to lose sight of our promised redemption. When our bodies fail, or our relationships sour, or our hearts betray us, we begin to wonder, "Is what's coming worth the wait?"

We need reminding of where we came from, and reassurance of where we are going. This is one part of the Holy Spirit's ministry within us:

> But if Christ is in you, although the body is dead because of sin, the Spirit is life because of righteousness. If the Spirit of him who raised Jesus from the dead dwells in you, he who raised Christ Jesus from the dead will also give life to your mortal bodies through his Spirit who dwells in you. (Romans 8 v 10-11)

The Holy Spirit is life, and what he has done for your soul is magnificent. Your eternal life has already begun, because Jesus has raised you to life through his Spirit and has come to live with you by his Spirit. Because we are born into a sinful world, our earthly bodies decay and die; but if the Spirit has given life to a soul, it will live in glory eternally. Not only that, the Spirit will "give life to [our] mortal bodies" when Jesus returns. We know he can do this because we know he has done this—when he raised Jesus physically from the dead.

Life forever with Jesus is our new reality, it has already begun, and it is a miracle of God's grace. For now, our resurrection life dwells in our mortal, decaying bodies. Things break. We sin. But one day, our resurrection life will enjoy resurrected bodies. The Spirit guarantees it.

## Putting Sin to Death

Whatever grips our minds controls our hearts, and then our actions. By reminding us afresh of the gospel—that the life we now have is Christ's righteous life—the Holy Spirit of God changes us to love what he loves and hate what he hates. He grips our minds with the gospel, purifies the affections of our hearts, and produces in us a holy life that desires to flee from sin.

> For if you live according to the flesh you will die, but if by the Spirit you put to death the deeds of the body, you will live. (v 13)

Would you say that you hate sin? That you most desire what brings glory to God? When was the last time you were convicted of a particular sin?

In seasons of pain, we can seize the opportunity of suffering—to flee from the sin that is often revealed in us by that suffering: pride, bitterness, anger that turns to resentment and rebellion against God, fear, and self-pity. We also need to confront the danger of suffering: it gives us a reason to ignore sin or excuse it away.

How do we understand this warning in light of the confident promise of new life that Paul wrote about earlier? If I sin, does that mean I lose Christ's gift of redemption? By no means! A new life in Christ means a secure life with Christ, but it also means a new heart producing Spirit-led desires. Those who have the Spirit dwelling in them simply cannot walk in a sustained, perpetual lifestyle of sin.

And those who have the Spirit dwelling in them now have the power to oppose their sin—to "put to death the deeds of the body." Fighting sin is both the Spirit's work and our work. We work, because he is at work. Our efforts are used by him, having been inspired by him, to change us.

We do not rely solely on ourselves, nor do we "let go and let God," but we confront and battle sin through the Spirit's enabling power. As the pastor John Piper put it, "Our working is not added to God's working. Our working is God's working" (*The Bondage of the Will, the Sovereignty of Grace, and the Glory of God*, April 13, 2016)

You can, and will, fight sin. The Spirit guarantees it.

## *Enjoying Being Children of God*

Suffering often causes us to doubt the love and care of God. Whether obvious and expressed ("If God really cared for me, he wouldn't allow this"), or a silent, brewing hesitation, these doubts lead back into fear, as we believe that our circumstances are somehow a result of our performance, our ability (or lack of it) to live a good, moral Christian life. We can therefore be tempted to believe that we don't deserve suffering, or that we do—that God is punishing us because we've been bad or we've done wrong.

But this is not the gospel:

> *You did not receive the spirit of slavery to fall back into fear, but you have received the Spirit of adoption as sons, by whom we cry, "Abba! Father!" The Spirit himself bears witness with our spirit that we are children of God ... provided we suffer with him in order that we may also be glorified with him. (v 15-17)*

God is your Father, and you are his beloved, adopted child through faith in Christ, apart from anything you have done. A sonship relationship with God means we will say when we suffer, "My Father still loves me, and he knows what he is doing. He may be disciplining me, but he is not punishing me. This suffering does not show that he does not love me, for his love for me was never based on my performance."

You can cry out to him with your doubts and fears, and you can lay your sin before him, knowing he will never reject or condemn you. You can depend on him as your involved, perfectly wise, tender-hearted, steadfastly loving Father, putting aside any notion that he is an aloof deity, or that he has targeted you out of spite. He has freely invited you into his family, so you can trust that whatever comes to you has been planned by him for your ultimate good.

You are, and will always be, a deeply loved child of God. The Spirit guarantees it.

## Help to Pray

In times of trials, our prayer life can suffer. When we don't know what to say—when we have no words to express our groans and cries—it's natural to feel we have no way to pray. It is in those moments that this ministry of the Spirit becomes precious:

> The Spirit helps us in our weakness. For we do not know what to pray for as we ought, but the Spirit himself intercedes for us with groanings too deep for words. (v 26)

When we don't know what to say to our Father because we are perplexed, defeated, weary, and joyless, we can trust that he knows our hearts, understands our needs, and is working through our weakness. We can trust this because the Spirit is putting words around what we cannot—taking our desperate tears and our conflicted feelings and turning them into the prayer we would have prayed if we were perfect!

So you can always speak to your Father, even when you have no words to speak. The Spirit guarantees it.

So yes, you are waiting, and yes, you are weak. But you are never alone. You can wait with dependence because the Holy Spirit tells you that God will make good on his promise to bring you home to him and, in the meanwhile, he will strengthen you to fight sin, assure you that you are a loved child of God, and help you to pray. The Spirit guarantees it.

# Reflect

~ How have you been relating to God lately? As your heavenly Father, who has given you his Spirit as a guarantee, or as a distant, disapproving God?
~ How does God's giving of his Spirit comfort you and help you persevere in hardship?
~ Knowing that the Spirit helps you pray, how will this truth affect your prayers?

# Pray

*Abba Father, how good and generous you are to give me your Holy Spirit. Thank you! I need him to reassure me of my coming redemption, to help me fight sin, and to teach me to pray boldly to you as my heavenly Father. I don't always yield to your Spirit; forgive my stubbornness, and help me to do that, with deep trust in all your ways. Intercede for me, Holy Spirit, with groanings too deep for words, especially when words fail me. You are my Father, and I love you. Amen.*

*For further meditation:* Psalm 139; 1 John 4 v 13-21

# Journal

CHAPTER TWENTY-SIX

# Good Soil for Growing Fruit

"He who has prepared us for this very thing is God, who has given us the Spirit as a guarantee"

2 CORINTHIANS 5 V 5

The Holy Spirit is given to every child of God—not to give us an easy life, but a changing character. As a living tree bears fruit, so a Spirit-inhabited person will also bear fruit.

Suffering, it seems, is often the soil that the Spirit uses to grow this fruit within us. To prepare that soil for growth, though, he often uses trials to draw out the true state of our hearts, exposing the layers of self-effort and perceived outward "goodness."

Have you ever heard someone (maybe yourself!) say, "I have always thought that I was a fairly patient person—until I had kids"? Or, "I never really struggled with anxiety, but since I lost my job and began battling health problems, I feel as though I've lost all peace"? Suffering has a way of revealing what lies deep within in us. Suddenly, when we find ourselves being pressed on all sides, sin that had been hidden begins to rise to the surface. Rather than continuing with the relatively patient, peaceful, and self-controlled life we've been able to maintain until now, we suddenly find ourselves struggling with anger, discontentment, anxiety, impatience, doubt, fear, bitterness, despair, or even hatred. We not only battle the trial itself, but the overwhelming battle of sin within us.

This, however, is why the guarantee of the Holy Spirit in every believer gives us the hope and courage to persevere. He will not leave us as we

KRISTEN WETHERELL & SARAH WALTON

are. In Galatians 5, Paul talks about what the Spirit is changing us into, as we seek to "walk by the Spirit," in line with his aims and work for us:

> But the fruit of the Spirit is love, joy, peace, patience, kindness, goodness, faithfulness, gentleness, self-control; against such things there is no law. And those who belong to Christ Jesus have crucified the flesh with its passions and desires. If we live by the Spirit, let us also keep in step with the Spirit. (Galatians 5 v 22-25)

Tim Keller, the pastor and author, highlights how attractive this is:

> To be "led by the Spirit" (Galatians 5 v 18) is to change, and be changed, to be the people we want to be. The Spirit-fueled development of Christ-like character is liberating, because it brings us closer to being the people we were designed to be, the people our Spirit-renewed hearts want us to be. (Galatians For You, page 151)

Through the rest of this chapter, we'll look at each segment of the fruit of the Spirit—what it is, how suffering can expose our lack of it, and how suffering can be the grounds for growing in it. I will be using John MacArthur's helpful descriptions in his ESV MacArthur Study Bible as we go through.

# *love*

> Agape love is the love of choice, referring not to an emotional affection, physical attraction, or a familial bond, but to respect, devotion, and affection that leads to willing, self-sacrificial service.

It doesn't take long to realize how conditional our human love can be. Whether it be in the context of a friend who wrongs us, a child who continues to walk in rebellion, or a spouse who becomes distant, our love can quickly fall short.

But we know what unconditional love is like, because we experience it each day in our Savior's dealings with us. And the Spirit works to show us that love, and then produce in us that love. And he can use the training ground of suffering to tear weak "love muscles" in order to stimulate the growth of stronger ones.

How have you seen your love fall short when you rely on your own strength to love others? Have you seen the fruit of love grow in you as you have grown deeper in your relationship with Christ?

## Joy

> [Joy is] happiness based on unchanging divine promises and eternal spiritual realities. It is the sense of well-being experienced by one who knows all is well between himself and the Lord. Joy is a gift from God, and as such, believers are not to manufacture it but to delight in the blessing they already possess.

Joy is surely the spiritual fruit that stands out most boldly in suffering since naturally, it would seem, suffering should produce the opposite of joy.

As we have talked about in several other chapters, suffering strips away our false sense of joy in the temporary things of this world. If our joy is located anywhere other than in the unchanging love of Christ for us, then suffering reveals that and steals that joy from us.

The Spirit is at work to give you joy in suffering—real joy, which is joy in Christ, and not in the circumstances around you.

Having the joy of Christ doesn't mean that we will never feel sadness or grief, and must always have smiles plastered on our faces, remaining unfazed by the myriad of disappointments, heartaches, and pain that we will inevitably face throughout our lives. That is not how Jesus lived on earth! However, as the fruit of joy grows within us, we are able to be genuine in the various emotions and experiences of life, while still having a confident joy in Christ and our promised eternity in his presence. We are battered by trials, but we are not left crushed or joyless in them.

Have you seen the Holy Spirit use your suffering to reveal ways that you have sought joy in something other than Christ? Have you struggled to find joy in your current circumstances? Ask the Spirit to increase in you a greater joy as your earthly hopes fade and your eternal hope grows.

# Peace

*[The] inner calm that results from confidence in one's saving relationship with Christ.*

Suffering has the ability to shake us to the core, rattling our confidence and comfort, often leaving us in a state of anxiety over what we can't control.

The Holy Spirit is at work to grow in us the peace that comes from knowing that we are not in control, but that God is—and that God is for us. He assists us to cast all our anxieties on God, and then to leave them there (1 Peter 5 v 7). He enables us to sleep at night because he reminds us that God never slumbers. Gradually, as Jesus Christ and his promises become our central focus, peace begins to drown out the noise of anxiety and fear.

Are you struggling to find any peace within your circumstances? Ask the Lord to grow the fruit of peace within you by the power of the Holy Spirit. He may not change your circumstances, but he will change you.

# Patience

*The ability to endure injuries inflicted by others and the willingness to accept irritating or painful situations.*

By nature, we are not patient people. We search for the quickest (and easiest) path to lose weight or regain health, we cleverly try to discern which line at the store will move the quickest, and we are easily frustrated when something causes a delay in our plans and expectations. The same is true in regard to our spiritual lives. Though we say we trust the Lord, impatience is quick to rise up when his ways don't match up with ours. Though God could answer each and every prayer in a moment, he often chooses to delay—not out of cruelty or indifference but out of a loving desire to grow the fruit of patience within us. Very simply put, we grow in patience through the practice of waiting. Therefore, as we learn to wait on the Lord—whether through persecution, seasons of long suffering, or our desire to grow in righteousness—the Holy Spirit will grow patience within us.

Have certain circumstances revealed a lack of patience within you? How have those same circumstances been used to grow you in patience? In what areas of your life do you need to pray for the Spirit's power to enable in you a Christ-like patience to bear fruit?

 ## Kindness

*[A] tender concern for others, reflected in a desire to treat others gently, just as the Lord treats all believers.*

Suffering will naturally create a hardness within us as we draw into ourselves, focus on our own problems, and become blind to or uncaring about others; but the Spirit will work in suffering to soften our hard hearts. Through him our suffering can prompt us to become more caring of others, and more sensitive to what they are walking through. The more we see the Lord caring for us in our time of need, the more we are willing to sacrifice our own time and comfort for the good of others.

Have you seen the Holy Spirit grow you in kindness as you are being changed through your suffering?

## Goodness and Faithfulness

*[Goodness is a] moral and spiritual excellence manifested in active kindness, and faithfulness is a loyalty and trustworthiness.*

We've already said that suffering provides an easy excuse to avoid obeying God. But the Spirit is at work to cause us to reject that thinking, and instead to love what God loves and hate what he hates. Along with that, we will be increasingly compelled to seek that which pleases the Lord and, in the power of the Holy Spirit, the fruit of goodness and faithfulness will flourish.

Have you seen your earthly desires fade as your desire for godliness has grown? If you are in the midst of a trial, I encourage you to look at your circumstances through the lens of what Christ desires to do in you through it. Rather than resisting what he may be allowing, would you ask the Holy Spirit to grow in you a greater desire for goodness and faithfulness?

## Gentleness

*[Gentleness or "meekness" is a] humble and gentle attitude that is patiently submissive in every offense, while having no desire for revenge or retribution. In the New Testament, it is used to describe three attitudes: submission to the will of God, teachability, and consideration of others.*

Suffering, unfair circumstances, and unmet desires can quickly reveal a belief that we deserve something better, causing anger, pride, and bitterness to take root in our hearts and rise to the surface. However, in God's grace, the Holy Spirit often uses suffering to grow the fruit of gentleness within us. It doesn't take us long to realize how miserable it is to live life filled with bitterness and resistance in response to what we can't control. That's the place in which to begin growing in submission and humility. As we choose to accept and rest in his control over our life, we begin to grow in gentleness toward both God and others. Only the power of the Holy Spirit can produce such fruit!

How have you seen the Holy Spirit increase the fruit of gentleness in your life? If you haven't, come honestly before Christ, asking the Holy Spirit to gently grow you in this area.

## Self-Control

*[Self-control] refers to restraining passions and appetites.*

Again, trials provide us with a ready-made reason not to keep a hold on our reactions and desires. Surely we deserve some pleasure and relief? But the Spirit works to show us that pleasure and relief lie in being self-controlled, because it is as we battle our sinful passions and turn from our selfish appetites that we find ourselves enjoying life as it was meant to be—a life obedient to the Lord.

Have your trials brought to surface a greater struggle with self-control as you battle against overwhelming and unfamiliar emotions? Do you find yourself overeating or attempting to numb your pain with unhealthy or sinful habits in response to stress, anxiety, or fear? Do you frequently lash out at those you love in response to feeling out of control of your circumstances? If so, will you bring these struggles to the Lord in honesty, asking for forgiveness and the ability to walk in self-control by the power of the Spirit?

## Fruit Grows

We must not expect to see perfection this side of glory. But we can excitedly expect to see fruit this side of it. As we "keep in step with the Spirit," the Spirit will be at work to grow his fruit. Fruit often grows slowly, almost unnoticeably, but grow it does, inevitably.

So look back. How can you see the Spirit growing fruit in your life? Are there any ways you've been seeking to thwart his work, rather than align yourself with it? Perhaps ask a Christian friend to help you see the fruit growing in your life. Celebrate the truth that God has not led you into a comfortable life, but he has changed you into a more Christ-like character. Ask him to help you grow in your ability to see the blessings of the Spirit's work within you, which will far outlive your present circumstances. Be praying that while you are planted in the soil of suffering, you will be growing the fruit of righteousness.

# Reflect

~ Do you see your life bearing the fruit of righteousness, even if it may be gradual? If not, ask a Christian friend what they can see. And if neither of you can see fruit growing, would you consider whether you have truly surrendered your life to Jesus Christ as your Lord and Savior?

~ If you are confident in your standing before God, but are still struggling to see the fruit of the Spirit in your life, would you prayerfully ask the Lord to continue to grow these nine fruits within you?

~ How have you seen Christ use your suffering to bear greater fruit within your life?

# Pray

*Lord Jesus, thank you that you have given me your Spirit as a guarantee that I am your child and have a home with you. I desire to reflect more of your character, but I constantly feel the pull of sin within me. By the power of the Holy Spirit, use these circumstances in my life to produce in me the fruit of the Spirit and a greater Christ-likeness. Help me to walk by the Spirit and grow in love, joy, peace, patience, kindness, goodness, faithfulness, gentleness, and self-control. Amen.*

*For further meditation:* Romans 15 v 13; 2 Corinthians 6 v 4-7; Ephesians 3 v 14-19

## Journal

CHAPTER TWENTY-SEVEN

# Resurrection Courage Right Now

"So we are always of good courage. We know that while we
are at home in the body we are away from the Lord, for we
walk by faith, not by sight. Yes, we are of good courage,
and we would rather be away from the body and at home
with the Lord"

2 CORINTHIANS 5 V 6-8

*H*ome. The word is full of meaning. For some of you, home brings
to mind warmth, stability, and rest; for others, it comes laden with
troubles and brokenness. Either way, home matters. Our past and
present senses of "home" affect us all, whether positively or negatively.

The Christian's ultimate goal is to be at home—at home with our Lord
Jesus: "We would rather be away from the body and at home with the
Lord." Our future home is a glorious one! But at the same time, Paul
shows us that what we do while we are "at home in the body," in our
present, matters.

To be "at home in the body" paints an important picture for us of a
meaningful embracing of and investment in the earthly lives God has
given us. Our days here are not without significance, Paul says, and they
can be lived courageously and confidently, even as we endure suffering. The expectation of our future home with Jesus propels us to courageously face whatever comes while we are at home in the body, even the
darkest of sufferings and the most broken of circumstances. Our faith
gives us hope. And future hope breeds present courage.

In other words, this day, right now, matters. The span of your earthly days matters. Your suffering in the midst of them matters. But equally, your present home is not what matters most.

If you allow your present home to matter too much, you will live "in the body" with caution and fear, trying your hardest to manage your circumstances and control your suffering—only to become increasingly frustrated, defeated, and afraid as life reminds you that you cannot control it. But if you live with eternity in mind, you can live courageously, investing your earthly time and making the most of opportunities you've been given, trusting the living Christ for the outcome and knowing this is not your final stop.

In this chapter, I'd like to focus on three areas from my own experience that have called for the courage that only comes from living with a sharp focus on my future home with Jesus. Each one is specific to my battle with chronic physical pain. These applications are not exhaustive, and I share them knowing that every person's story looks different. My hope is that they will help you apply God's word to your circumstance of suffering, so that you may live courageously by faith while "at home in the body."

## The Courage to Pray Specifically

As I bow my head and close my eyes to pray, I open my mouth to speak—but no words come. The pain throbbing in my body distracts me, and the sheer load of needs overwhelms me. I'm at a loss to know which hardship to address first. I think of Sarah, who hurts in her own way, and I feel burdened by the needs I could bring to God solely between the two of us—not including the many other people we know and love who are hurting in their own ways.

During this time of stillness before the Lord, I freeze up and I doubt. The temptation lingers to play it safe, to limit my prayer requests to those I know will be answered in the affirmative, and to filter my cries because the realities feel... too messy. I doubt my ability to bring anything to God that makes sense, as my mind feels so distracted and dominated by the pain.

In these moments, I need resurrection-life courage. I need to remember that in the presence of Jesus, there will be no more tears or pain—so I can pray for healing, for myself and others, knowing it will be answered in an ultimate sense, if not in this life. I need to remember that God is for me and has proven this through the gift of his beloved Son to give me a home with him—so I can pray with openness and honesty. I need to remember that I have an enemy who will try to deceive me and cause me to fear, but who has been defeated by the risen Christ—so I can fix my eyes on Jesus even while I'm at home in the body.

It takes courage to bring our requests to God, not knowing what his answer will be, or how long we will be away from him. But we need only to ask, to pray specifically and courageously for healing, deliverance, strength, and help because our eternal home with Jesus is real, and it's where we are headed. If our Father does not answer our prayers while we are at home here, we can know that he will accomplish an ultimate deliverance from suffering whenever we go to be in the presence of Christ.

## The Courage to Obey Boldly

As I write this, I'm fighting for courage to trust and obey the Lord. Three months ago, a searing discomfort ignited in my neck and jaw. But every x-ray and examination have looked picture-perfect, making this new pain an enigma. No one knows what's causing it, and no one knows if and when it will stop. Pleasures I enjoy—singing, talking, eating—now come racked with discomfort.

What scares me the most, though, are the speaking engagements I've committed to. How can I possibly fulfill them when talking for five minutes causes me pain? What if I'm forced to cancel or hand them off to someone else? The fear of what's coming paralyzes me. I don't want to obey. I want to run.

In these moments of faint-heartedness, I need resurrection-life courage. I need to remember that God has promised to raise my soul and body to an eternal home, caring for my greatest need—so he will surely care for me in the details of this temporary one. I need to remember that though the body will break, Jesus reigns eternally—so I can depend on him for strength and endurance now, and hope in the redeemed body to come. I need to remember that Jesus defeated sin along with all its bodily fruit, like fear, worry, and disobedience—so I can choose peace, trust, and submission, knowing that someday sin will be no more. I need to remember that Jesus is in control of this day and every day, and he will give me all I need to obey him, though it may not be all I would like to do. I need to remember that he delights in me, and he does not demand from me what he does not empower me to give.

It takes courage to obey Jesus when the road ahead looks daunting and our home away from him feels like anything but home. But we need only to trust and obey him in this moment, to let him take care of tomorrow, to hope in a final home that endures forever. Because our eternal home with Jesus is real, and it's where we are headed, we can walk by faith when we cannot see, knowing that he sees everything and will uphold us until we get there.

## The Courage to Give Generously

Another doctor's visit means another withdrawal from our savings account, and another five-hour road trip for a day spent at their offices. Every time we see the doctor, my husband and I learn to hold a bit more loosely to earthly assets like money, time, and energy. But I admit that I occasionally find myself thinking about all the earthly riches that would be ours had Lyme disease not been God's plan for us.

In these moments, I need resurrection-life courage. I need to remember that with Jesus I have treasures at home in heaven and spiritual riches now that nothing on this earth can compare with—and this gives me courage to be open-handed with the resources he has entrusted to me while I'm in the body. I need to remember that God has been infinitely generous to me through his mercy and grace, promising me an eternal home—that he won't withhold the good things he knows I need while I wait for it.

It takes courage to let go of earthly gain and give generously—particularly when suffering has shown us how uncertain our immediate future is. Suffering depletes us of resources, and we could cling tightly to time, money, and energy to preserve them all for rainier days. But our eternal home with Jesus is real, and it's where we are headed! The One who gave his life so that we will live forever at home with him is the One who will provide for us while we are at home in the body. He will provide for our rainy days, one way or another; and he will bring us to a place where rainy days are no more. We are free to be generous to our church, to other Christians, and to strangers because, in Christ, we have everything we need.

## Live with Courage

It's natural that you would rather be away from the body and at home with Christ. Cling to him by faith, and someday your home will be everything God intended it to be and everything you long for it to be. While you are at home in the body, you can live with prayerful, obedient, generous courage because your confidence is in the Person who rules and reigns forever, and who will one day take you to the place you will eternally call "home."

## Reflect

~ What particular circumstances, desires, or requests will you pray about specifically today? How does healing in the ultimate sense encourage you to ask for temporary deliverance?

~ How is God asking you to obey him boldly, despite your limitations and understanding?

~ What is one way you can give generously today? How does the reality of your heavenly home with Jesus encourage you to give?

# Pray

*Father, how I long to be at home with you! Yet, I thank you for the gift of being at home in my body right now. I trust your good plans for me: that you have me here for a purpose, to invest in this temporary home with good courage and confidence in what's coming. Open my eyes to see how you would have me live courageously for your glory. Point out where I am withholding confidence in you and shrinking back in prayer, obedience, and generosity. Thank you for raising me to new life! Help me to live in the light of your Son's resurrection today. Amen.*

*For further meditation:* Luke 22 v 39-46; 2 Corinthians 5 v 11-21; Ephesians 3 v 14-21

# Journal

CHAPTER TWENTY-EIGHT

# God Can Handle Your Emotions

"So we are always of good courage. We know that while we
are at home in the body we are away from the Lord, for we
walk by faith, not by sight. Yes, we are of good courage,
and we would rather be away from the body and at home
with the Lord"

2 CORINTHIANS 5 V 6-8

*S*uffering tends to rock the very foundation on which Christians
stand—our faith.

This is not because our foundation in Christ is unsteady, but
because our feet are slippery. As we struggle to "walk by faith, not by
sight"—as we struggle to trust what we cannot yet see—we will wrestle
at times with the doubts and questions that arise from our lack of sight.
You may know it is true that Christ is good and that he reigns, and that
Christ has prepared a home for you with him, but your emotions may
well be feeling something very different about him and about your future. What do we do when our emotions seem faithless?

## Wrestling with God

Meet Job, who endured more pain than most will in a lifetime,
while having absolutely no understanding of the heavenly battle being
waged over his life (he was not given the insight we are given in Job 1
v 6-12 and 2 v 1-7).

Job felt his pain, and wrestled with God as he cried out in his anguish:

*[God] set me up as his target;*
*his archers surround me.*
*He slashes open my kidneys and does not spare;*
*he pours out my gall on the ground. (Job 16 v 12b-13)*

Consider what Job is saying here. He is accusing God of pitilessly crippling him. He is charging the Creator of the universe with deliberately, almost maliciously, targeting him. How could he accuse the Almighty God with such a bold statement? Why was he not struck dead for not only thinking such a thought, but verbalizing it?!

I'm sure many of us have known a time when the burdens of life seemed more than we could bear, only to experience yet another crushing blow. I know I have felt the same as Job did during seasons when it seemed as if I had a target on my back. Do you ever struggle with thoughts that God seems either absent or else is the one orchestrating circumstances which bring you flat on your face in anguish? Do you ever feel hurt with, confusion about, and even anger toward God stirring within you because you can't understand how a loving Father could allow such pain? Do you ever wonder what to do with those feelings— where to turn with these raw, hard questions?

God says, *Bring it to me. Tell it to me. Pour it out to me. I am big enough to handle your feelings toward me.*

In *The Gospel of Job*, Mike Mason writes:

*How much better it is for a believer in God to exhibit a rough exterior than to bottle things up inside a tawdry, saccharine layer of Christian "goodness." (page 184)*

During a long season of my son's illness ravaging our home, I came to a point where the burdens became so exhausting that they began to wear on my heart, face, and words. The pain had broken through my façade of strength, and every word I spoke came from a place of weariness, brokenness, and confusion. I could no longer manage anything beyond simply clinging to the little faith I had. My family was not my own, my future was not my own, my life was not my own. Of course, this really had been true all along, but it wasn't until I was faced with a reality I never would have chosen for myself that I was forced to grapple with the deep and hard questions of my faith. The blessing, however, of reaching the point of being unable to bottle it all up is that I poured out my frustrations, confusion, anger, questions, doubts, and fears to the Lord. I could no longer come to him with neat and tidy prayers or a heart of genuine praise and thankfulness. I was a raw mess, struggling to make sense of my faith and my feelings. And I was exactly where the Lord wanted me to be—pouring all of myself into his gracious, loving, merciful arms. He didn't necessarily make sense of my circumstances, but he taught me to trust his goodness and sovereignty over what I couldn't understand.

That's exactly what Job was given as well. He was never given answers as to why he was suffering, but he was given a greater glimpse of God—which was enough to humble and encourage Job through circumstances he couldn't understand. The LORD answered Job:

> *Can you lead forth the Mazzaroth in their season,*
>   *or can you guide the Bear with its children?*
> *Do you know the ordinances of the heavens?*
>   *Can you establish their rule on earth?*
> *Can you lift up your voice to the clouds,*
>   *that a flood of waters may cover you?*
> *Can you send forth lightnings, that they may go*
>   *and say to you, "Here we are"?*
> *Who has put wisdom in the inward parts*
>   *or given understanding to the mind? (Job 38 v 32-36)*

In those depths, and in our honesty, something amazing can happen. As we began to let the muddy waters of our hearts run more freely, we often begin to see untruths that we have been believing, as well as many truths of the gospel that we may never have fully grasped or properly appreciated. The more we bring our mess, honest questions, and emotions to Christ, the more he reveals to us not only the flaws of our own hearts, but the true beauty of his.

This is what led Job to respond to the Lord in both humility and awe:

*I had heard of you by the hearing of the ear,*
*but now my eye sees you;*
*therefore I despise myself,*
*and repent in dust and ashes. (Job 42 v 5-6)*

## Come to Me

God can handle our mess. He can handle our hard questions—even our faithless ones. It is not wrong to feel like this. But it is wrong to wallow there. Christ is not someone to whom we simply vent our emotions and then walk away just as lost; rather, he wants us to come to him honestly and walk with him in greater freedom.

*Come to me, all who labor and are heavy laden, and I will give you rest. Take my yoke upon you, and learn from me, for I am gentle and lowly in heart, and you will find rest for your souls. For my yoke is easy, and my burden is light. (Matthew 11 v 28-30)*

Jesus invites us to come to him honestly, not superficially. He is willing for us to give him our burdens and questions—but he wants us to receive from him, too. "Take my yoke upon you," he commands. In these verses, we are given four simple steps to handle our messy, overwhelming, questioning emotions...

1. *Bring your sin, pain, questions, and messy, raw emotions to Christ,* the only One who is sufficient to handle and do anything about it.

2. *Take his yoke upon you.* Following Christ, even when suffering comes, is where true freedom is found. As we affix ourselves to Christ, letting him take the lead, we will find that life under his lordship is far more restful than life "free" of his lordship. Rather than remaining distant from him, believing we will find joy and freedom apart from him, we can trust that everything we endure under his sovereign hand will not be wasted, but will be used to make us supremely satisfied in him and will bring him glory through it.

*3. Learn from him.* Having brought our honest questions into the open through prayer, we must then listen to Christ by searching the Scriptures for the promises he has given us. An honest question is willing to listen to a truthful answer. I encourage you to make a list of any questions you may be wrestling with, ask Christ to open your eyes to the truth, and then make a list of as many Scripture passages as you can find that speak of God's promises to you in response to those questions. If you aren't too familiar with reading the Bible, ask a Christian friend to do this alongside of you. I have found this practice incredibly humbling, encouraging, and insightful.

*4. Find rest.* We cannot save ourselves; but we do not need to. Jesus has taken the weight, pain, and consequences that our sins deserve onto himself in order to give us forgiveness, freedom, life, and hope, as we walk through life and on into eternity affixed to him. If we keep trying to save ourselves, we will continue to walk burdened by the exhaustion and pressure of the effort, or by the sense of defeat over the circumstances that we cannot control and the problems we cannot fix. Rest in the ups and downs of life is found as we grow in our true understanding of our identity in Christ, which allows us to come honestly before our Father as his deeply loved children. He knows our hearts, he knows our needs, and he longs to give us rest.

## No Need for a Bottle

Friend, you don't need to settle for, or strive for, a façade of Christian goodness, bottling up the feelings you think "good Christians" shouldn't feel and trying to present a neat and tidy front to God. It's exhausting for you, and distances God from you. Your God says, "Come." Your God says that you can pour it all out to him.

As we learn that we're free to be real with Jesus, we're able to learn to be real with people around us too. The world doesn't need to see more people who seem to have it all together; it needs to see real people with real struggles, real emotions, and a real hope. Being real with people starts with being real with our Savior. So as you seek to walk by faith and not by sight when what you can see looks overwhelming to your faith, come to Christ in honesty, laying down every doubt, question, and emotion before him, trusting that though he may not give you answers, he will give you rest.

## Reflect

~ Do you believe it is wrong to bring our questions and emotions to the Lord? If so, would you read through the book of Job and David's psalms, with a willingness to learn from their honesty and the realness of their faith?

~ Who do you trust with your doubts and questions? Are you willing to bring them all to Christ and allow his truth to speak into every area of your heart?

~ If we can't bring our burdens to him, then where do we have to turn? Will you trust that Christ is strong enough to handle even your hardest questions?

## Pray

*Lord Jesus, I want to be strong and unwavering in my faith, but as I endure this pain and watch others suffer around me, I wrestle with questions of your goodness, sovereignty, and purpose. I feel confused and angry. Thank you that you want me to come to you with these feelings. Thank you that you are willing to listen to me in all my conflicting thoughts and feelings. Thank you that when I don't know how to put it into words, I don't need to. And thank you that you reply by inviting me to trust you, to remember your promises, and know rest. Please point me to the promises I need to know, and give me the faith I need to trust them. Please help me to walk by faith, until the day that I am at home with you and my faith becomes sight. Amen.*

*For further meditation:* Job 10; Job 13 v 15; Job 23; Psalm 42; Psalm 102

## Journal

CHAPTER TWENTY-NINE

# When God Doesn't Seem Good

"So we are always of good courage. We know that while we are at home in the body we are away from the Lord, for we walk by faith, not by sight. Yes, we are of good courage, and we would rather be away from the body and at home with the Lord"

2 CORINTHIANS 5 V 6-8

It was a vacation I desperately needed. I really, really needed to relax, unwind and recover.

So I had been anxiously awaiting this vacation, in dire need of catching my breath from the hardships and stresses in life, which were greatly wearing on my body and spirit. As the day approached for our departure, I pleaded with the Lord for good health and a restful time away.

We made it to our destination and I was so thankful that we had stayed healthy and arrived to enjoy our vacation. I thanked God for his goodness and took a deep sigh of relief!

The next morning my daughter woke up extremely sick.

I was devastated. "Please protect the rest of us. Please would none of the rest of us get sick," I prayed.

Two days later, I came down with it as well. Now my prayers were no longer full of thanks for God's goodness:

*"Why, Lord? Don't you see that I need a break?!"*

As I lay on the couch while the rest of my family ran off to the beach, I felt angry and confused at why God would allow this. Didn't he care how beaten down I was? I believed that God is good, but this did not feel good. I felt a battle in myself, not wanting to grumble and complain, and yet struggling with doubts about God's goodness.

Haven't we all experienced a time when something painful happens that we can't make sense of, often far worse than a temporary illness? A life-altering disease or injury, the death of a loved one, a lost job, a broken relationship, years of a seemingly unanswered prayer; these things can challenge us to the core about who God really is—whether we really believe God is good and faithful.

Consider the young couple who are faithfully seeking the Lord and longing for the blessing of a child, and yet struggling with why God is allowing their battle with infertility to continue. Or the pastor who, at the great cost of leaving family and security, obeyed the Lord's leading and embarked on the journey of planting a church in unfamiliar territory, only to end up closing its doors after only a year. Or how about the time when it seemed as if God had opened the door to a desired home or a perfect job when, suddenly, the home was bought out from under you or the job opportunity was given to someone less qualified? There are moments in our lives when circumstances simply don't make sense. In fact, some circumstances seem downright cruel.

We will all face these moments in our lives, when what we believe about God will come face to face with circumstances that don't seem to line up with what we believe; when everything we can see tells us that God is not good to us. At those moments, whether we realize it or not, we ask ourselves this question: Do we believe God is good by what we see or do we believe God is good because of who he is?

I have often tried to shape God into a God who fits with what I can see, reducing him to a God that I am comfortable with and can make sense of, instead of trusting the truth of who he is, and accepting what he has allowed as his good and perfect will.

I appreciate Lydia Brownback's insight in regard to this struggle:

*God often acts contrary to how we think a good God should act. The
answer we think we need seems so logical and clear to our way of thinking, yet God does not provide it. That is where faith comes in. Real
faith isn't the belief that God will do a particular thing; real faith is the
conviction that God is good, no matter what he does and however he
chooses to answer our prayers. God always has our best in mind, and
he works to bring it about, no matter how it may look initially to our
way of thinking. (Trust—A Godly Woman's Adornment, page 30)*

# Living by Faith in the God of the Cross

There is no greater example of this than the cross of Jesus Christ.

> *But it was the LORD's good plan to crush him
>    and cause him grief.
> Yet when his life is made an offering for sin,
>    he will have many descendants.
> He will enjoy a long life,
>    and the LORD's good plan will prosper in his hands.*
>                                    *(Isaiah 53 v 10, NLT)*

God's plan was to crush his own Son. That certainly doesn't sound
like something a good God would do, until we realize that his will was to
crush his own Son in order to save us—sinners in rebellion against him.
Although Christ's death caused him unimaginable pain and sorrow, it
was ultimately a part of fulfilling God's good purpose in defeating sin
and death, freeing us from eternal pain and sorrow.

Think about what you would have seen had you been there on the
first Good Friday. You would have seen God's Son crucified in agony,
killed by his enemies. You would have seen a Father God not coming to
the rescue of his dying Son. You would have seen evil winning. But now
think about what you would have known by faith, if you had had Isaiah's
words in your mind. You would have known God's Son was being crucified in agony as part of the good plan that he and his Father had devised
before creation. You would have known that his death was an offering

for sin, a perfect sacrifice being made on your behalf, so that you need not face judgment. You would have known that mercy had won.

The very heart of our faith tells us that circumstances will not always make sense and God will not always explain everything to us; that faith often tells a very different, and better and truer, story than sight.

As I saturate myself again with the truth about Christ's incredible sacrifice on the cross as part of God's plan to save sinners like me, I'm so thankful that he does what is good in his eyes, and not mine. We may never fully understand the pain we experience while on this earth, but we must run to the truth that he has proven his goodness in the greatest way possible through Christ's death and resurrection. We can choose to trust in that same goodness even when we can't make sense of the circumstances we face:

> For my thoughts are not your thoughts,
>   neither are your ways my ways, declares the LORD.
> For as the heavens are higher than the earth,
>   so are my ways higher than your ways
>   and my thoughts than your thoughts. (Isaiah 55 v 8-9)

## Faced with a Choice

As I lay on the couch on vacation, feeling miserable while my family enjoyed the beach, I had two options. I could walk by sight and allow what I couldn't understand to simmer into a rolling boil of anger toward the Lord, or I could choose to walk by faith by reminding myself that God's ways are higher than my ways, and that he is trustworthy and good, even when I can't make sense of my circumstances.

Friend, this life is filled with circumstances that will leave us questioning or even denying God's goodness if we live by what we see, rather than by faith in what God has promised. The choice we face is a daily one. We can choose to either trust what we see and define what's good for us ourselves, and grow annoyed with God and doubt his goodness; or we can live by faith in a crucified Savior and let him define what's good for us, even if it means exercising our faith muscles as we choose to trust him over what we can see and feel.

So let's come to Christ with our doubts and weaknesses, and ask him to give us the faith to take our eyes away from what we can see in front of us and lift our eyes again to the cross—because that is where we will find assurance and confidence in the undeserving goodness and faithfulness of our heavenly Father. Is God good? Yes. He died for you.

## Reflect

~ Are there currently circumstances in your life that make it seem as though God has not been faithful? How can you hold those up in light of the gospel this week?

~ Has there been a time in your life that you can look back on in which you can see God's past faithfulness and goodness when, at the time, it seemed otherwise?

~ Will you choose to trust who God is rather than what your feelings may be telling you?

## Pray

*Lord Jesus, as the psalmist prayed, "Be gracious to me, O Lord, for to you do I cry all the day. Gladden the soul of your servant, for to you, O Lord, do I lift up my soul. For you, O Lord, are good and forgiving, abounding in steadfast love to all who call upon you. Give ear, O LORD, to my prayer; listen to my plea for grace. In the day of my trouble I call upon you, for you answer me. There is none like you among the gods, O Lord, nor are there any works like yours. All the nations you have made shall come and worship before you, O Lord, and shall glorify your name. For you are great and do wondrous things; you alone are God." Amen. (Psalm 86 v 3-10)*

*For further meditation:* Hebrews 10 v 23; 1 Thessalonians 5 v 23-24; 2 Thessalonians 3 v 3; Titus 3 v 4-7

## Journal

CHAPTER THIRTY

"So whether we are at home or away, we make it our aim
to please him. For we must all appear before the judgment
seat of Christ, so that each one may receive what is due for
what he has done in the body, whether good or evil"

2 CORINTHIANS 5 V 9-10

This seems like a strange passage with which to end this book. I
remember getting to these verses and thinking they felt out of
place. Up to this point, Paul has written on the light of the gospel,
on treasures in jars of clay, on the inner self being renewed through
affliction, on our heavenly home with Christ...

... and suddenly, the judgment seat. What are we to make of this?!
In all the verses we've covered, Paul has written to Christians, to people who have seen the light of God's glory in the face of Christ, people
who desire to live courageously in the midst of affliction until faith turns
to sight. And Paul is still writing to these people when he says:

> We must all appear before the judgment seat of Christ, so that each one
> may receive what is due for what he has done in the body, whether good
> or evil. (2 Corinthians 5 v 10)

Christians will be judged for what they have done while in the body.
Judgment Day is not only for unbelievers, but for God's people, too. And

this, as much as any of the other verses that we've looked at, transforms how we respond when we suffer.

## ✳ *Our Judge Is Our Savior*

The judgment seat is a reality that we often don't talk about, either because we are unaware of it or we aren't sure how to reconcile it with other biblical truths. But we need to talk about it, because every Christian will stand before the Lord Jesus Christ to be judged. This is not a truth we should ignore or neglect, because it has implications for how we live right now, and because it gives us gospel clarity on our standing before God.

First, the implications for how we live now. Suffering friend, Jesus will judge the way that you handle your afflictions when you stand before his throne. Doesn't knowing that change the way you want to respond to them? How you steward them? How you prepare for them? We'll draw out these applications in a moment, but for now the point is this: Jesus, the Savior, will be our Judge, and he will examine all the good and evil we have done and reward us accordingly.

Second, our standing before God. You may be asking, "Does this verse mean I can't be sure of my salvation?" A wonderful question, and the answer is, *You can be sure, and you should be sure.* Paul writes 11 verses later:

> *For our sake [God] made him to be sin who knew no sin, so that in him we might become the righteousness of God. (5 v 21)*

Your standing before God, your acceptance into his family, is not what this verse on the judgment seat addresses. Rest assured, if you trust Christ for salvation he has taken your sin, and he has given you his righteous perfection, and you will never be rejected or eternally condemned.

So when someone who trusts Christ appears before his judgment seat, to receive "what is due for what [we have] done in the body," Paul is talking about judgment-reward, not judgment-condemnation. Because the Judge is also our Savior, the judgment will be about whether our lives have brought him pleasure and glory, and not about whether our lives have earned us eternity. That gives us hope in our suffering, and changes how we live in our suffering.

## Your Body and Your Rewards

While the reality of the judgment seat affects the whole scope of our lives, Paul's context ties the judgment of believers to the sufferings they've experienced while living in the body. Afflictions of any intensity are a trust given to us by God. So, as brothers and sisters entrusted with unique sufferings, we examine ourselves to see what we are doing with them, and whether that is good or evil.

*How you are preparing for suffering matters.* Preparing for sure affliction means soaking in God's word and pursuing faithfulness to him right now. Are you making the most of your time? Investing yourself in what is good and true? Are you preparing for intense sufferings by clinging to God in the mild ones and when life seems to be running smoothly without any sufferings at all?

*How you are responding to suffering matters.* When suffering of any intensity comes, how do you react? We've written much in this book about the difference between suffering well and suffering poorly, of responding in the way the Spirit would lead us or responding in sin. How will you handle the trust of affliction in both outward actions and the hidden places of your heart?

*How you are using your suffering matters.* What is God teaching you through suffering? How are you sharing this with others? What unique opportunities of gospel witness and acts of good courage is he entrusting to you in the midst of the hurt and pain?

Consider what you have done and what you are doing in the body, whether good or evil. Someday, before Jesus' judgment seat, you will give him an answer to these questions and you will receive what is due to you for these things. Eternal life is not a reward, because it's a free gift; but there will be rewards in eternal life.

# Our Motivation

But we mustn't stop there. If 2 Corinthians has taught us anything, it's that the hope of the gospel transforms our hurt. But it also transforms our motivation to please Jesus in the midst of it.

John Piper tells a story to illustrate the two ways we can be motivated:

> *Duty is good, but delight is better. Picture me bringing a dozen roses home to my wife on our wedding anniversary. I hold them out to her at the door; she smiles and says, "Oh Johnny, they're beautiful, why did you?" Suppose I lift my hand in a self-effacing gesture and say, "It's my duty..." (desiringgod.org/articles/there-is-no-greater-satisfaction)*

Duty and delight are opposite motivators. Duty produces white-knuckled attempts to do the right thing for the sake of doing the right thing, because we ought to, and is stripped of joy. Delight produces acts of love, joy, and sacrifice that aim to please the one for whom they're intended, because we want to.

When Paul writes, "We make it our aim to please him," he's referring to the motivation of delighting Jesus. Yes, the reality of the judgment seat motivates us to please Christ, but that motivation will only produce white-knuckled duty if it's not allied to gospel-motivated delight. We are only able to please Jesus because of his gospel and the new desires it produces within us. Because I know Christ's death won forgiveness and freedom for me, I can please him in how I live, and I will want to please him in how I live.

So we do not aim to please him out of duty, as if we must begrudgingly earn our entrance into eternity. We aim to please him because it's our delight to spend our lives making much of him and showing him to others.

The day of judgment, then, becomes a day of joy—a day to anticipate with eagerness. Think of it: you will stand before Jesus, your resurrected Lord and Savior, finally seeing him. And for each moment you were faithful in your suffering you will hear him say to you:

> *Well done, good and faithful servant ... Enter into the joy of your master. (Matthew 25 v 21)*

Whatever other rewards your service brings you, to have that ringing in your ears for eternity will surely be the greatest!

## Hope When It Hurts

So, friend, as we close our time together, I'd love for you to ask yourself:

~ Have I entrusted my soul to Jesus for eternity, or am I letting my suffering tear my faith and love from him?
~ Have I entrusted my suffering to Jesus, so that I aim to grow in love for him and dependence on him during this time I'd never have chosen?

It's as we entrust our souls and our suffering to Christ that we discover real hope—not just hope for our future, but hope in our present, to wrestle with and work out and trust in God's purposes in our suffering. With Christ, there is hope, even when—especially when—it hurts:

*For God, who said, "Let light shine out of darkness," has shone in our hearts to give the light of the knowledge of the glory of God in the face of Jesus Christ.*

*But we have this treasure in jars of clay, to show that the surpassing power belongs to God and not to us. We are afflicted in every way, but not crushed; perplexed, but not driven to despair; persecuted, but not forsaken; struck down, but not destroyed; always carrying in the body the death of Jesus, so that the life of Jesus may also be manifested in our bodies. For we who live are always being given over to death for Jesus' sake, so that the life of Jesus also may be manifested in our mortal flesh. So death is at work in us, but life in you.*

*Since we have the same spirit of faith according to what has been written, "I believed, and so I spoke," we also believe, and so we also speak, knowing that he who raised the Lord Jesus will raise us also with Jesus and bring us with you into his presence. For it is all for your sake, so that as grace extends to more and more people it may increase thanksgiving, to the glory of God.*

*So we do not lose heart. Though our outer self is wasting away, our inner self is being renewed day by day. For this light momentary affliction is preparing for us an eternal weight of glory beyond all comparison, as we look not to the things that are seen but to the things that are unseen. For the things that are seen are transient, but the things that are unseen are eternal.*

*For we know that if the tent that is our earthly home is destroyed, we have a building from God, a house not made with hands, eternal in the heavens. For in this tent we groan, longing to put on our heavenly dwelling, if indeed by putting it on we may not be found naked. For while we are still in this tent, we groan, being burdened—not that we would be unclothed, but that we would be further clothed, so that what is mortal may be swallowed up by life. He who has prepared us for this very thing is God, who has given us the Spirit as a guarantee.*

*So we are always of good courage. We know that while we are at home in the body we are away from the Lord, for we walk by faith, not by sight. Yes, we are of good courage, and we would rather be away from the body and at home with the Lord. So whether we are at home or away, we make it our aim to please him. For we must all appear before the judgment seat of Christ, so that each one may receive what is due for what he has done in the body, whether good or evil.*

*(2 Corinthians 4 v 6 – 5 v 10)*

# Journal

# Acknowledgments

Where do we begin? How do we adequately thank all the people who've done for us far more than we can see? A simple mention must suffice for now, though our thanksgiving for all of you far surpasses what this page can contain.

From day one, the incredible team at The Good Book Company has believed in this project with unwavering support and passion. What began as a self-produced book intended solely for our church, you gave wings to serve suffering saints everywhere. Thank you for catching this vision and believing in us.

Carl, you are brilliant, our British friend! You've not only been our editor-extraordinaire, but our advocate. Thank you for laboring alongside us, considering our weaknesses, pushing us, focusing us, and always turning our gaze back to Christ. You are a gift to the body, and to the literary world. We are better writers, but more importantly better sufferers, because of you.

Our love for Christ's gospel is largely due to The Orchard Evangelical Free Church. Pastor Colin Smith's word-filled preaching (with all its ripple effects throughout the Orchard body) has deeply influenced our teaching. Your pastoral faithfulness, Pastor Colin, means the world to us.

We must acknowledge the medical team at Fox Valley Wellness Center in Wisconsin. Though our earthly tents are being destroyed, you are bolstering them through your phenomenal practices and care. The Lord has used you.

To our friends: Thank you for praying faithfully for our physical and spiritual endurance throughout the writing process and beyond, and for the words in this book. You are the hands and feet of Jesus to us.

To our families: The steadfast love of Christ has been your anthem over us as we've suffered and written this book. Your prayers and service for us, and your sorrow and rejoicing along with us, we have treasured in our hearts.

To our husbands, Brad and Jeff: You are our comforters. In all our affliction, and throughout the writing process, you have demonstrated "the Father of mercies and God of all comfort, who comforts us in all our affliction." You have read and re-read drafts, and been our sounding boards. You've told us to rest when the pain was too much. You've spurred us on when we felt like giving up. You have shown us Jesus Christ. We love you, our dear husbands.

To my (Sarah's) kids, Ben, Hannah, Haley, and Eli: Thank you for your patience with me throughout this process. I know your young hearts and minds struggle to understand the point of all of this pain in your lives, but I pray that you will one day proclaim the truths of the gospel and come to love Jesus and glorify him through what appears so hopeless. Though I often fall short, I love you with every ounce of my being.

Lord Jesus, we adore you. You are our peace, our joy, our light. You are our hope. May you be glorified in these imperfect pages.

# EXPLORE

## BY THE BOOK

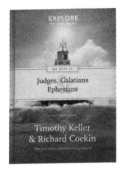

Join Timothy Keller and Richard Coekin as they lead you verse by verse through the gripping days of the judges, the gospel freedom of Galatians, and the Christ-centered glories of Ephesians. Their helpful questions, insightful explanations and prompts to apply God's word to your life will take you to the heart of God's word and then push it deep into your heart.

Timothy Keller and Sam Allberry take you through three key New Testament sections. Experience the joy of the gospel in Romans. Wrestle with the challenging applications of James' letter. And listen to the Lord's teaching the night before he died, as recounted by John.

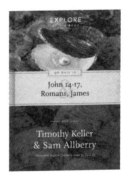

Allow Mark Dever and Mike McKinley to sit alongside you as you open up your Bible day by day. Enjoy the treasures of Ruth, Jeremiah and 1 Corinthians as you explore the Bible, book by book.

## www.thegoodbook.com/explorebythebook

# thegoodbook
### COMPANY

*Opening up the Bible*

At The Good Book Company, we are dedicated to helping Christians and local churches grow. We believe that God's growth process always starts with hearing clearly what he has said to us through his timeless word—the Bible.

Ever since we opened our doors in 1991, we have been striving to produce resources that honor God in the way the Bible is used. We have grown to become an international provider of user-friendly resources to the Christian community, with believers of all backgrounds and denominations using our Bible studies, books, evangelistic resources, DVD-based courses and training events.

We want to equip ordinary Christians to live for Christ day by day, and churches to grow in their knowledge of God, their love for one another, and the effectiveness of their outreach.

Call us for a discussion of your needs or visit one of our local websites for more information on the resources and services we provide.

Your friends at The Good Book Company

| | | |
|---|---|---|
| **NORTH AMERICA** |  thegoodbook.com |  866 244 2165 |
| **UK & EUROPE** | thegoodbook.co.uk | 0333 123 0880 |
| **AUSTRALIA** | thegoodbook.com.au | (02) 9564 3555 |
| **NEW ZEALAND** | thegoodbook.co.nz | (+64) 3 343 2463 |

 **WWW.CHRISTIANITYEXPLORED.ORG**
Our partner site is a great place for those exploring the Christian faith, with a clear explanation of the good news, powerful testimonies and answers to difficult questions.

ISBN 978-1-78498-073-3

**Hope When it Hurts**
ISBN: 9781784980733